NEW, REVISED EDITION

Exegetical Method

A STUDENT HANDBOOK

Otto Kaiser • Werner G. Kümmel

EXEGETICAL METHOD

EXEGETICAL METHOD

A Student's Handbook
New Revised Edition

OTTO KAISER
and
WERNER G. KÜMMEL

Translated by
E. V. N. GOETSCHIUS
and
M. J. O'CONNELL

THE SEABURY PRESS · NEW YORK

1981
The Seabury Press
815 Second Avenue
New York, N.Y. 10017

Printed in the United States of America

Library of Congress Cataloging in Publication Data

Kaiser, Otto, 1924–
Exegetical method.

Translation of Einführung in die exegetischen
Methoden.
1. Bible —Criticism, interpretation, etc.—
Addresses, essays, lectures.   I. Kümmel, Werner,
Georg, 1905–   joint author. II. Title.
BS531.K313   1981   220.6   81-477
ISBN 0-8164-2303-2 (pbk.)   AACR1

CONTENTS

Otto Kaiser

✤ ✤ ✤

OLD TESTAMENT EXEGESIS [1]

I   The Task of Exegesis

In both the Old and the New Testaments the Bible bears witness to the presence and action of God in the world and among human beings. In so doing, it helps bring about the rule of God and communion with him.[2] Though God is hidden by the ambiguities of the human person and the world, the word in which he expresses his presence and action lays claim to being itself an action of God. This is precisely the claim that finds expression in talk of the Bible as the *word of God,* whereas the position of the Bible as the document constitutive of the Church's faith finds expression in talk of it as *sacred scripture.* In the Church's re-presentation and ever-new defense of the testimony of scripture in her teaching, her profession of faith, and her action, she bears witness that through scripture and the proclamation based on it she becomes aware of God's reign and of communion with him, in order then to spread both of these to the entire human race.[3]

An examination of the history both of the Church and of theology shows (1) that the process of re-presenting the biblical testimony is an unending one; (2) that the process is constantly in danger of separating itself from its constitutive basis; and (3) that the plurality of testimonies threatens to create ambiguity regarding that which they attest. It follows from (1) that there is no *theologia perennis;* from (2) that there must be theology in the sense of a methodical, disciplined reflection of the testimony on itself in the form it takes at any given moment; and from (3) that in fulfilling its task in a concrete community this self-reflection must be conducted in terms of the community's confession of faith.[4]

It is in this theological context that the development of *biblical exegesis as a critical historical science,* resulting from the modern growth of historical consciousness, is to be located.[5] It is historical because its aim is to re-present a textual meaning formulated in the past. It is critical because it ignores all traditional opinions on the texts as well as the apparent meaning of the texts themselves, and goes behind these to search out the real horizon actually present in them. In principle, therefore, it owes its understanding of these texts entirely to its own inquiries. Unlike precritical exegesis critical historical exegesis does not begin with the hermeneutic question of the meaning of the texts for the present time whether in terms of faith-acceptance or of systematico-theological reflection or of practico-theological application. Rather it asks the *historical question of the meaning the biblical text has within its original horizon of meaning.*[6]

But in order that the testimony of scripture may be truly heard and in order that a real encounter with this testimony may follow upon this hearing, it is essential to proceed without bias, strange though this may sound at first and, in the last analysis, limited though this requirement must be. The interpreter must first be prepared to suspend the dogmatic convictions of the Church, the traditional views of scholarship, and even his own understanding of the faith in order to listen with true objectivity to the text that lies before him.[7] The much misunderstood saying, that it is the task of the interpreter to understand a writer better than he understood himself, is applicable here only in the restricted sense that the exegete is obliged "to explain the background out of which the expression concerned has arisen."[8] Understood in this way, the requirement is perfectly consistent with that of an unbiased, impartial exegesis, that is (since scripture deals

with matters pertaining to the past), of critical historical exegesis.

In the framework of a basic introduction to the methods
of critical historical exegesis, it cannot be our task to pursue
hermeneutic problems in general or the problems involved in
a Christian understanding of the Old Testament in particular.[9]
For the student, the first question, quite part from the question of what religious and confessional tradition he has grown
up in, is how to become acquainted with the methods of procedure that are of crucial importance in exegesis and with the
scholarly resources that are at his disposal for pursuing these.

But if we are to be able to situate and evaluate correctly
the task and practice of exegesis, we must have a *basic understanding* of the hermeneutic problem. We will then see
that the distinction between the critical historical and the hermeneutic approaches can only be a matter of varying emphasis and not of complete separation. The objective basis for
this assertion is both the *nature of the text* and the *character
of human understanding*. A text is a formal, schematic structure whose linguistically coded message necessarily contains
elements of vagueness that prevent the intention of the author
and the reception and concretization of this intention by the
reader from being identical.[10] In any case, the author's intention and the reader's perception of it cannot be identical but
only congruent when the text in question is a literary one (in
the most comprehensive sense of the term *literary*). The understanding of a text, therefore, is always determined by the
horizons of both author and reader.

The work of exegesis can uncover the prior knowledge
that the text presupposed in its original readers, as well as
the underlying intellectual presuppositions of that age, which
were taken for granted; these form the horizon of meaning
proper to the text. But in this process, not only the prior
knowledge that the interpreter possesses and the tools that he
has at his disposal but also his own objective grasp of exis-

tential problems (a grasp resulting from his self-understanding and his vital experiences) play an inevitable role.[11] This is all the more true when the interpreter is faced with the task of correlating the horizon of reality of the text with his own so as to ensure an appropriate understanding of the text.[12]

At this point, it is obvious that exegetes must *cooperate* with the practitioners of the other theological disciplines. Since exegetes are wholly taken up with the solution of their own philological and historical problems, they must seek instruction in the problems of understanding in general and of contemporary faith-inspired understanding in particular, either from a special discipline of *hermeneutics* or from *systematic theology* as the two purveyors of the conclusions reached by philosophical and empirical hermeneutics. *Church history* also plays a part as the source of information on the transmission of biblical faith down to the present time.[13] A similar program would be suggested by reflection on the problems that arise in attempting to answer the question of the contemporary significance of the Old Testament for Christian faith.[14]

If exegesis is to achieve its goal of re-presenting the biblical testimony, the exegete himself must keep in mind *the connection with the discussion of scientific theology as a whole*. Only thus will he be able, as a competent reader and a competent Christian, to draw the boundary lines for the re-presentation of that testimony in the present. His ability to do so will be the crowning result of his critical historical interpretation, but it will also be a function clearly differentiated from the latter. In all this, however, the Old Testament exegete must also keep in mind the question of how his particular text fits into the entire process of formation of the biblical tradition, and whether the concrete message of his text is confirmed by the New Testament message or corrected by it or superseded by it in principle.[15]

Critical historical work and the pursuit of the biblical

sciences generally enjoy different degrees of popularity at different times. This fact causes no problem as long as exegetes do not think they can do without the systematic and practical disciplines and as long as the devotees of the latter for their part do not forget that the neglect of exegesis leads to the degeneration of theology, the impoverishment of preaching, and, ultimately, the surrender of the Church to fanaticism.[16] Since the critical use of scientific literature on the Bible presupposes a knowledge of its methods, it is desirable that every theologian learn these methods. It must also be kept in mind that the scientific consultation of biblical texts for secondary purposes, i.e., for purposes of general history, the history of religions, sociology, and other disciplines, requires a prior exegetical expertise.

II Text of the Old Testament: Textual Criticism

A reliable, critically edited text in the original language forms the general basis of every scholarly pursuit connected with the Old Testament as well as the obvious basis for exegetical work. We have such a text in the *Biblia Hebraica,* edited by Rudolf Kittel (3rd ed., 1937), and now in the *Biblia Hebraica Stuttgartensia,* edited by Karl Elliger and Wilhelm Rudolph (1966–77). Both editions are based on the oldest completely preserved manuscript of the Hebrew Bible, the Codex Leningradensis, which dates from the year A.D. 1008.[17] Along with this, one should make use of a translation that satisfies scholarly requirements, such as we have in the *Heilige Schrift des Alten Testaments* of E. Kautzsch and A. Bertholet,[18] or the Zürich Bible. In using the second of these, the reader must be aware that the division of chapters and numbering of verses differs to some extent from that of the Hebrew Bible.[19] The nonbiblical Jewish writings that are important for exegesis are translated in E. Kautzsch (ed.), *Apokryphe und Psuedepigraphe des Alten Testaments;*[20]

R. H. Charles (ed.), *The Apocrypha and Pseudepigrapha of the Old Testament;*[21] E. Riessler (ed.), *Altjüdiches Schrifttum ausserhalb der Bibel;* W. G. Kümmel (ed.), *Jüdische Schriften aus hellenistisch-römischer Zeit;*[22] and the *Texte von Qumran* in E. Lohse's bilingual edition.[23]

First of all, we get a *preliminary feeling* for the text to be interpreted by reading it aloud several times, and then we make a *rough written translation* that will serve as the basis for further work. The definitive translation comes only after all exegetical methods have been applied, since the text we are working with will be modified by textual criticism, and the meaning of the words will be rendered more exact in terms of their context by exegesis both of the individual words and of the overall context. By reading the text aloud repeatedly, we should become so familiar with it that any interpretation we may afterwards give it will really be an interpretation of the text and not of our rough translation or of some other version. Repeated reading brings out the initial questions that affect the understanding of the text, and the preliminary basic approaches to be taken; these, together with our own prior knowledge, form the horizon of problems for further study.

The basic aids we make use of are, first, a scientific Hebrew lexicon that gives an adequate supply of forms to help us determine the one we are dealing with and an adequate picture of the range of contextually determined meanings a word may have, and, second, a scientific grammar.[24]

Further work will be facilitated if, as the case requires, we determine not only the basic meaning or possible meanings of a word but, at the same time, the variant meanings that might apply in the context so far as we can determine this last at this preliminary stage. Finally, we should not be satisfied in principle until we have a clear understanding of the points of grammar and syntax in the text.[25]

The next step in exegesis is the recovery of the text, or

textual criticism. Since the Old Testament writings or parts of them were diffused in manuscript form for 1,500–2,000 years, we must reckon with the usual unconscious distortions and deliberate alterations that take place in the course of such a tradition and with which we are familiar from our own practice in copying. It follows from this that the text to be explained must first be established. In the ideal case of a scientific edition of the text (such as Kittel's edition and the *Biblia Hebraica Stuttgartensia* endeavor to be), one will take into account all the available witnesses to the text in the original language and in the translations made during the period of manuscript diffusion, using the oldest complete manuscript in the original language as a basis.

However, the student in his own exegetical work will usually have to be, but also can legitimately be, content to use, along with the Hebrew text, appropriate editions of the Greek and Latin Bibles, i.e., the Septuagint and the Vulgate,[26] and, if occasion demands, the Samaritan Pentateuch[27] and the scrolls and fragments discovered in the desert of Judea.[28] In addition, the student can indirectly gain information on the state of the Aramaic, Syriac, and Arabic translations by using Brian Walton's Latin translation of the London Polyglot. To some extent, the *Polyglot* takes still other traditions into account, and devotes four monumental volumes to the Old Testament; the critical apparatus is in the sixth volume. However, the fact that it was published in the seventeenth century already shows that its value for textual criticism today is rather limited.[29]

Methodically reliable work in textual criticism presupposes a knowledge of the *history of the Hebrew text and its translations,* as this is set forth to some extent in introductions to the Old Testament[30] and, of course, in specialized works.[31] A survey of the history of the text and the available editions, and an introduction to textual criticism are given by Martin Noth, *The Old Testament World,*[32] and especially by

Ernst Würthwein in his indispensable workbook, *The Text of the Old Testament*.[33]

Textual criticism proceeds in three steps: the *collection* and arrangement of the variants; the *examination* of the variants; and, finally, the *determination*. In the first step, the variant readings found in the manuscript tradition are arranged in the order in which they arose in the history of the text.[34] Here it is necessary to note only such variants as are neither intentional alterations nor later assimilations to the Masoretic Hebrew text. It is immediately clear, of course, that this judgment itself presupposes a knowledge of the specific character of the witnesses to the text. The student must derive this from the specialist literature,[35] but at the same time he must not neglect to make a full translation not only of the primary Hebrew text but also of the other witnesses to the text being used. Lest the student overlook any variant, he will find it useful to write down the witnesses one after another. In this context, a special problem arises from the divergence, in the books from Joshua to Kings and in Jeremiah and Ezekiel, between the Masoretic text and the Septuagint, and in Judges between the Codex Vaticanus and the Codex Alexandrinus as well. A shorter text in the Septuagint that strikes one as being the original text may, after a study of several chapters, prove to have been abbreviated at a later stage. Great care must therefore be taken in dealing with such divergences.

At this step it is also necessary to separate out mechanical scribal errors. The material collected and found relevant must now be examined on the basis of linguistic evidence and the evidence of the subject matter. Here the Masoretic text, as it appears in the Stuttgart edition, deserves very careful attention. If considerations appear against it, the range of meanings of doubtful words is first of all to be investigated lexically; then the linguistic usage is to be examined with the help of a Hebrew concordance, especially Solomon Mandelkern's *Veteris Testamenti Concordantiae Hebraicae et Chaldaicae.*[36]

A similar procedure should be followed in regard to the Greek variants. Not only must the range of meanings of a Greek word be determined,[37] but investigation should be made of its Hebrew equivalent(s). Here the work of E. Hatch and H. A. Redpath, *A Concordance to the Septuagint and Other Greek Versions of the Old Testament,*[38] is as indispensable as Mandelkern's, since after each Greek word (in its proper lexical order) Hatch and Redpath list the Hebrew equivalents, indicating which equivalent (if there be more than one) is used for each occurrence of the Greek word.[39] Before it is concluded that a Hebrew phrase cannot be rendered in Greek, the parallels must be examined and looked up in the Hebrew concordance.

Metrical and genre-critical grounds for challenging the text will appropriately be considered only in the course of a subsequent metrical investigation, if such is relevant, and in the course of literary criticism. The latter is usually distinguished from textual criticism as "higher" from "lower." In general, and despite many bad examples they may encounter, students should make it a rule carefully to separate lower criticism and higher criticism, textual criticism and literary criticism. Given the complexity of the problems connected with the Old Testament text tradition, it is not surprising that many people give up on their attempt to define clearly the goal of Old Testament textual criticism. For a number of reasons that need not be developed here, it will be most practical to aim at the form of the text that was regarded as canonical in rabbinic Judaism ca. A.D. 100.[40]

While Old Testament textual criticism thus understood seeks to establish the form of the text that became canonical in Judaism, the aim of literary criticism is to establish the literary unity of the text as being primary or secondary. But even though the distinction between textual criticism and lit-

erary criticism deserves unconditional respect, a certain
amount of overlapping with regard to the exegesis of details
and context is unavoidable in the examination of subject matter that is sometimes required in textual critism. There is always occasion for this examination when an individual word
or an entire phrase does not seem to fit into the context,
whether *context* be taken in the narrow sense of the immediate text or in the broad sense of the Old Testament world. It
is already clear at this point that the individual steps of exegesis must be taken up in a definite order, but that because
the context constantly leads to overlappings the presentation
of the results of the exegesis must follow the order and arrangement dictated by the overall purpose.

In determining the value of witnesses to the text, one
will, in accordance with the goal established above, always
give preference to the Masoretic text when this does not
prove impossible on grounds of language and content and
when the first- and second-century Jewish witnesses to the
text show it to be canonical. Only if the Masoretic text is
untenable are the other witnesses to the text to be taken into
account. The Hebrew text is always to be corrected in accordance with these if sufficient grounds for the originality of
their variants can be produced. Only when none of the variants has any claim to being the original is it admissible to
emend the texts by means of a conjecture. Unless one can
successfully reconstruct the path from the hypothetical reading to the form of the text as we have it now, it is better to
indicate in the translation that the text is obscure than to fill
in with an uncertain conjecture and thus pretend to an objectively unwarranted certainty. The information and considerations that are important in making a decision should be indicated in the final presentation along with the decision itself,
as the nature of the study may require. The resultant departures from the original text are to be worked into the translation and signified as such by the use of diacritical marks.

Given the limited goals of textual criticism, it may be that some of the departures from the Masoretic text will have to be studied once again in the context of literary criticism and redaction criticism.

III Literary Criticism and Redaction Criticism

Since an understanding of a literary work as the coherent and finished composition of a particular author is lacking in the Old Testament period at least until well into the Hellenistic age, we must reckon with the fact that the individual books of the Old Testament and the units within them (the texts) are not primary compositions. They are rather collections and revisions of earlier traditions, some of which were oral traditions that may under certain conditions have already acquired a finished linguistic form. Frequently, too, they are made up of documentary sources and more or less extensive strata that have undergone previous revision and into which at times independent traditions may well have been incorporated. This description applies primarily to narrative literature, but probably, or even demonstrably, it also applies in an analogous way to the collections of songs in the Book of Psalms and in the Song of Solomon, to the collections of sapiential sayings and reflections in the Books of Proverbs, Qoheleth, and Job, and, obviously, to the prophets.

Therefore, it cannot be assumed without proof that a single Old Testament book or a single one of its texts[41] is an original unity. This situation determines the task of literary criticism. In dealing with individual texts, literary criticism asks what the original content is and what expansions there are. In regard to an entire book or a continuous narrative, it seeks to determine what the work's original content is or, if the situation calls for it, what the original content of its sources is, what the various strata are that have undergone revision, and what additions of detail have been made. In both cases, literary criticism seeks to elaborate a picture of the genesis of the text. Insofar as literary criticism also determines the prevailing viewpoint of the text, it passes over into *redaction criticism;* insofar as it takes into account the historico-temporal aspect, it becomes *redaction history.*

The work of literary criticism begins by *determining the limits* of a text, to the extent that such a determination is needed. In doing so, it passes critical judgment on the divisions that the pre-Masoretic, Masoretic, or modern exegetical traditions have introduced into the text.[42] A basic knowledge of the genres of Old Testament literature is a further prerequisite.[43] In keeping with the current results of research in literary criticism, tradition history, and genre history, the assumption is made that the individual story is older than the narrative sequence and that the individual reflection, legal disposition, or prophetic oracle is older than the series of proverbs, string of reflections, series of laws, or legal or prophetic books. Artistic narratives such as we have in the history of the succession to David's throne, in the Books of Jonah and Ruth, and, to some extent, in the Book of Esther raise problems of their own. Furthermore, we must take into account the fact that in the psalter originally independent songs have been joined with others or have been divided up.

In separating a text from a continuous story, the way in which it is connected with what precedes and what follows must likewise be determined. In many cases, this question of the connection of a text with the preceding and following texts cannot be limited simply to the immediately preceding and following texts, because sections that were originally closely connected may very likely have been separated by redactional work. If clear evidence of content and form points to the independence of the text, the examination of the connections at its beginning and end may supply at least some preliminary standpoints for understanding the composition of the book or the method followed by the narrator or redactor in his work.

Structural analysis is the second indispensable step that is basic for literary criticism and the subsequent identification of genre and exegesis of the text in its entirety. It is indispensable as well for any text that is definitely primary, such as a self-contained individual story, a psalm that has remained intact, or a prophetic oracle that has not been subjected to revision. Such an analysis ascertains the structure of the text, that is, its internal arrangement.[44] In the process, we glimpse ways in which the text may have been disturbed, and these will enable us to infer secondary influences. In practice, our procedure is to take the text, once it has been distinguished from what precedes and follows, and to work through it repeatedly, dividing it by scenes, strophes, and/or functions, in order then to elucidate the functional connections of these structural components, which is to say, the points of view that were at work in the composition of the whole. Since this last point will be important especially in the determination of the genre and in the exegesis of the whole, it is sufficient at this point to conduct the analysis at a relatively formal level and, in the case of a story, to distinguish introduction, body, and conclusion from one another. In dealing with other genres, the components may be much more complex.

Working through the text a second time, the student traces the train of thought by dividing it into small units from sentence to sentence. If he comes upon unusual syntactical phenomena that have not already been elucidated when making the rough translation or doing the textual criticism, he will now protect himself against hasty conclusions in literary criticism by consulting a work on syntax or, if need be, and in the ideal case, by making his own investigation.

In this process, especially if the student works through

the text repeatedly over a period of time, doublets, secondary expansions, and glosses, alternations between poetry and prose, stylistic deviations, omissions, shifts in thought, and even direct contradictions will be brought to light if any are present.

The observations made can be further grounded if the structural analysis is preceded or followed by a *linguistico-syntactical* analysis at the level of sentence and text. This begins with an identification of the type of sentence used in each case as a nominal, verbal, or inverted verbal sentence. Then the student observes the retrospective references by means of the enclitic personal pronouns and the prospective references by means of verbs that initiate action (command, wish, request, and variations of these),[45] questions, sentences stating purpose, as well as shifts of subject and object, reintroduction of a subject as an object, and so on. With the help of an appropriate tabular arrangement of the results, the student obtains a formal structural scheme that enables him to correct and check a structural analysis based on comprehension of content.

In the work of genre identification, the procedure just described (which is that of Wolfgang Richter, slightly modified) will probably prove to be of only limited help, since, being primarily of a descriptive linguistic character (despite the structural emphasis added at a second stage), it is limited in its capacity to meet the standards of linguistic textual analysis. A point that should not be overlooked is that the fulfillment of the reasonable requirement so emphatically laid down by Richter, namely, that the *linguistic aspect* (*form*) of the text be methodically integrated into the interpretation, is still only in the experimental stage, as is to be expected in view of the present state of linguistic inquiry.[46]

On the basis of this and, if necessary, a further stylistic and metrical analysis, the *real work of literary criticism* begins. First, the obvious glosses are eliminated. In addition, a determination is made, if needed, of whether these glosses are from one or several hands. Next, the basic text is isolated. In the process, the composite character of the text may well become evident. Furthermore, the additions that remain after the removal of the glosses and the isolation of the basic text are classified according to their homogeneity, and put into a probable sequence.

The results of this literary criticism now become the object of *redaction criticism*. This determines whether the given section of text is perhaps the work of a redactor and thus a composite product. Redaction criticism also endeavors to ascertain the purposes operative at the various levels of redaction and to place them in a temporal sequence. Since these two tasks are normally possible only in connection with the interpretation of content, any results at this point will for the moment be of heuristic character.

In an ideal kind of scholarly investigation, a whole book or continuous work will be analyzed in this fashion before a reliable judgment can be made on the sources used and the strata of revision.[47] A beginner, however, will be content with setting forth his limited findings and with formulating the approaches these suggest. Finally, without detracting from the scientific character of his work, he can compare his results with the various possible interpretations that are discussed and defended in the history of research and decide which of the previously defended hypotheses is most consonant with his own observations. For information, he may turn to the introductions and the monographs listed therein.[48] In the exegesis of the text in its entirety, the results of literary criticism are to be integrated in such a way that the text under consideration is explained from each stage of its development to the next. In the process, the results of redaction criticism will be applied in a specific way.

It should be clear, in view of what has been said, that literary criticism and redaction criticism are no more ends in themselves than textual criticism is, but are rather essential keys to the understanding of the text.

IV *Linguistic Description or Form Criticism*

Style and Metrics

In the context of interpretation, the stylistic description that is the next step is concerned in the last analysis with determining the intentions that guided the author in his choice of linguistic devices.[49] In thus describing our task, we must however be clear in our own minds that style was not as much a matter of free choice for the Old Testament writers as it is at the present time; style was largely determined by the existing genres themselves. Stylistic analysis and genre identification are thus implicitly connected with one another.

On the other hand, we must be conscious of the limited extent to which, as people of a different culture and language, we can fully appreciate stylistic devices. In cases of doubt, then, we will do better to reserve final judgment rather than produce a psychologistic novel instead of a functional stylistic analysis. In addition, the field of Old Testament stylistics was neglected for an uncommonly long time as compared with other exegetical approaches and was really only rediscovered by the representatives of the "interpretation of the work" approach.[50]

The linguistic character of the text may in some cases already be the object of linguistico-syntactic analysis in connection with the study of structure that prepares the way for literary criticism. If not, then we can study it now, with emphasis on the identification of the types of sentence and the determination of which type predominates and why. We should observe whether monologue or dialogue predominates in the case of discourse; whether report, description, argumentation, or instruction predominates in the case of narrative; whether statements are chiefly assertions or requests. Thus we obtain a basic set of objective functional characteristics.

The sparing use of the article and the so-called *nota accusativi* should tell us that we are dealing with an *archaic* style; the increased use of these points to a *later* style. The sparing use of locative, temporal, qualitative, and quantitative specifications indicates a *concise* style; the increased use of these a more *ample* style. In stories, the presence of a later and more ample style is indicated by the presence, for example, of two or three acting persons and the naming of secondary figures.[51]

The presence of striking figures in the areas of sound[52] and form[53] and of unusual expressions in the area of word and phrase,[54] if these be appropriate or frequent, shows that we are dealing with an *artistic style*.

Finally, it is recommended that at this point the entire significant vocabulary of the text be checked against a concordance as a means of having our attention called to the writer's use of distinctive expressions and of formulas from everyday life and from literature. By a *distinctive expression,* I mean here an expression that repeatedly occurs in the same work or the same literary stratum and that goes back to the author of the text (insofar as this can be determined and insofar as its individuality, as compared with a body of material that admittedly represents only a very small part of the language once spoken, leads us not to expect its derivation from colloquial language). By a *formula,* on the other hand, I mean an expression that repeatedly occurs in other works or strata.[55]

In the case of a formula, we must determine whether it belonged to colloquial language or to a specific *genre style.* We can reckon with the first alternative if the formula is found in texts from various genres and if no borrowing of motifs or modification of genre can be shown. We can reckon with the second alternative if the formula is linked to a specific genre and at the same time frequently serves as a motif.[56]

Obviously, this kind of work calls for an extensive knowledge of the findings of Old Testament literary and genre criticism or else for a no less sizable expenditure of effort in order to gain the required competence in the subject by checking with the pertinent introductions, monographs, and commentaries. This stage of our work is of decisive importance for subsequent stages. The observation of genre style and the listing of numerous parallel passages will be rewarded when the time comes for determination of genre, and the observations made regarding vocabulary will prove their worth in the semantic analysis to be made in the course of detailed exegesis. If we encounter identical or similar motifs elsewhere, these will be of profit in connection with the investigation of the history of the material, a subject that is likewise best introduced when semantic analysis is taken up. Finally, in checking the vocabulary against a concordance, we will also most readily be made aware of the composite character of a text or its *mosaic style,* that is, a style that results from working with pieces borrowed from literature.[57]

If we look back now, we will clearly see that the work of stylistic criticism, which was not especially attractive when we started it, is more rewarding than we expected. In addition to the points already made, the determination of a style as popular and derived from colloquial speech or, on the other hand, as artistic prose, or of a specific genre as connected with a particular social stratum will prove helpful in the effort to locate a text in relation to social background and history.

Until now, I have said nothing of a special and not unimportant aspect of stylistic study: the rhythmical shape of the text. I certainly need not defend the inclusion of this aspect in our study.

Every language has its natural *rhythm*. Each speaker uses this in an individual yet flexible way to express his emotions and intentions. In the process, linguistic convention shows him the way he must go if he is to be understood. Since the genres are to be regarded as linguistic conventions, it is clear that metrical analysis, which is in fact a part of stylistic analysis, is likewise connected with the determination of genre. Each of the steps we are taking is thus bringing us closer and closer to the goal we have been pursuing for some time now: genre criticism.

But first let us understand the problem of metrics. In a particular instance, a speaker may follow the stylistic laws governing a recurrent rhythm; then, depending on the degree of rhythmization we will speak of a *rhythmical prose* or, if the regularity imposes itself on us, of *verse* or, less accurately, of poetry. The underlying pattern is called the *meter*.

A recurrent pattern is obtained by the repetition of some dominant element. In Hebrew (I suppose here the correctness of the view that the Hebrew system is *accentual,* based on natural word-stress), this means the prominence given to one syllable by accenting it. In Hebrew, as in Arabic, accent is "less a matter of increased loudness (as in German) than of a higher pitch (a musical accent, not an accent by means of expiration of breath)."[58] Meter is based on rhythmical motifs, for example, a double anapest ($\cup\cup'|\cup\cup'$). The tried-and-true basic model for Hebrew metrics is the *Qinah* (dirge) with its $3 + 2$ accented syllables. Other important combinations are $2 + 2$, $3 + 3$, $2 + 2 + 2$, and $3 + 4$ or $4 + 3$.

Our basic difficulties in dealing with the metrics of Old Testament texts are due to several facts: that we have these texts only as already equipped with a secondary system of vocalization that was established by the Masoretes 1,000–2,000 years after the emergence of the texts; that in our theorizing we must entirely depend on reconstruction; and that in cases which are dubious and yet very important

for literary criticism we encounter only too frequently the occurrence of mixed meters and consequently have difficulty in
forming a judgment. In handling problems of metrics, we are
forced to walk a path between an exaggerated optimism and
an equally inappropriate pessimism. In any event, if observations based on meter are used in the formation of judgments in literary criticism, they must be shored up with further arguments.[59]

The presentation that follows upon an analysis of style
and meter should, as in the preceding and following steps of
the overall work, be limited to a communication of relevant
findings with clearly stated questions and clearly drawn conclusions. The exegesis must not be turned into an exercise in
boring pedantry by striving for a completeness of information
that is disproportionate to the results it yields.

V Genre Criticism and Genre History

As a rule, neither in scholarly literature on the Old Testament nor in the other scholarly disciplines dealing with literature is any termino-logical distinction made between the
form and the *genre* of linguistic formations. Thus scholars
speak indifferently of form criticism and genre criticism,
form history and genre history. However, given the widening
range of sciences that have been dealing with linguistics in
the last few decades, there is something to be said for limit-
ing the concept of *form* to the linguistic expression found in
a concrete text or external form. A well-developed linguistic
description that takes adequate account of individual text
forms and their concrete realization will perhaps some day be
able to give an appropriate description of the various kinds of
texts as a linguistic supplement to the genres. In this way,
the results of such a description would become relevant for a
genre study that considers the associated specific processes of
communication in their concrete historical context. But as

long as this desirable point has not been reached, genre study must be content to make what observations it can of texts as organized in relation to the intentions of their authors, and of the ideal schema, the *genre,* which each text embodies in a pure or modified form.[60]

The task of genre determination, or *genre criticism,* arises from the fact that every individual linguistic utterance antecedently bears the mark of linguistic convention. As a system of speech that has developed through history, a language places certain schemata at the disposal of those who express themselves in this language; these schemata are adapted to the particular intention and situation of the speaker and enable him more easily to make himself understood by others as a result of their shared ability to express themselves in a particular concrete language. We make frequent use of such schemata every day, as, for example, when we use set formulas of greeting in welcoming and taking our leave of the people we meet or when in beginning and ending our letters we use set formulas that are in keeping both with our relationship to the recipient and with what we have to say. If such letters were presented to us without indication of the situation in which they were written, we could within limits identify the situation because of our knowledge of certain characteristic expressions. The limits to which I refer would evidently change as we attempted to move from a determination of the generic situation to a determination of a more specific situation in which formulas are more nuanced and current rules established by society are being applied.

If we try to draw a definition from these admittedly terse considerations and observations, we may describe a *genre* as the schema of a linguistic structure, a schema precontaining a specifically organized linguistic form for use in achieving a specific communicational goal in a specific situation or, as biblical scholars since Hermann Gunkel's time usually put it, in a specific *Sitz im Leben* ("situation in life").

In dealing with the Old Testament, we usually do not know the author and the speaker with whom he is probably identifying himself (at least as a member of the same group) in specific linguistic utterances, nor, if we also take into consideration the preliterary stage of oral tradition, do we know the circle of persons who stand at the beginning of this tradition or at any point along its history. Consequently, in our area of investigation, genre study is important not only for purposes of systematic literary description but also for determining the *Sitz im Leben* both of the genre and of the individual texts belonging to the genre. Such study also makes it possible to form hypotheses regarding the group, the addressees, and their sociological location. In this way, Old Testament literature both as a whole and in the units that make it up is linked to the concrete historical life of Israel and Judaism; for the investigation does not stop at the individual text and the determination of its genre with the help of comparison and analogy. It extends rather to the *history of the genre,* then the *history of institutions, traditions,* and *motifs,* and finally to the *history of Israelite and Jewish literature.*[61]

Within this overall framework, *genre history* provides the history of the individual genres and of the transformations these have undergone in the course of their history, including any changes that may have occurred in the relation of their *Sitz im Leben* to what Georg Fohrer calls their *Sitz im Buch* ("their situation in the book"). In investigating this history, sound method requires taking the individual unit as the starting point in almost all the books of the Old Testament and asking whether its *Sitz im Leben* was primarily oral or primarily literary and whether the genre that is given concrete embodiment here is being used in its original form or in a modified form. The typical example of a genre used in a modified form is the *Qinah* or dirge[62] used as a prophetic oracle conveying threats or scorn (compare, for example, 2 Sam 1:19ff. with Amos 5:1ff. and Is 14:4bff.).

As examples of the primarily literary use of the genres of lamentation of the people and of the song of thanksgiving, I will risk suggesting the much discussed city songs in the so-called Apocalypse of Isaiah (24:7ff.; 25:1ff.; 26:1ff.).[63] If the student is to recognize the signs that something is secondary, he must first have studied the structure, the motifs, and their functional interrelationships in cases where the genres are found in a pure form with a primary *Sitz im Leben*.

It is clear that the presence of a pure genre is at the same time a criterion of relative age and that the presence of a mixed genre is a sign of later origin. The problem of age is nonetheless significantly complicated by the consideration that the Israelites entered into the heritage of the great cultures of the ancient Near East and Egypt after their migration into Canaan (at the latest) and that part of this heritage was fully developed genres in the areas of law, religion, and cult; furthermore, the Israelites continued to be in constant contact with neighboring cultures. In addition, a particular liturgical situation may have led, at a very early date and, in certain circumstances, even primarily, to a composition that borrowed its elements from various cultic genres. The situation is reversed when the student of genres confronts the problem of a motif being isolated and developed into a new and independent genre.

As an example of a composite Israelite composition that is presumably very ancient, the Song of Deborah in Judges 5 may be suggested. An example of a genre that arose from giving independent existence to a particular motif is the song of confidence, which developed from the confidence motif in psalms of lamentation or supplication (compare, for example, Ps 23 with Ps 56:45).

Since the term *motif* is used in every possible context, let me explain the concept: a literary *motif* is "a recurring, typical and thus humanly significant situation" that is developed in linguistic form by means of concrete *traits* that are in part conventional and specific to the motif and in part individual.[64]

If we look back now at the points I have been making in the immediately preceding passages, it becomes clear that in the determination of a genre we must take into account not only the timeless, ideally typical aspect but also the diachronic (or historical) and, if the state of research allows it, the synchronic (or parallel) aspects as well.

The process of *genre determination* includes two steps. In the first, the structural analysis is reviewed and, with the help of a comparison with the textual organization uncovered at the stage of literary criticism, is, if occasion requires, refined through consideration of functional viewpoints. The student must now pay more careful attention to relations between units of meaning, between formal units, between strophes if he is dealing with verse and such considerations become relevant, and, above all, between motifs. In narratives, it is already desirable at this point to reduce the sequence of actions to as brief a statement as possible, thus clarifying the schema that literary scholarship calls the basic story (*Fabel*).[65] In this step we should likewise attempt to establish the *theme,* i.e., the message the author intends to convey, as distinct from the action.[66] These determinations will help us attain the goal, which is to grasp as accurately as possible the special character and intention of the texts being studied. In summary, every genre has a characteristic structure and genre style of its own, but these can be learned only by means of detailed studies.

If a text with its particular form has no analogues in its own or a related linguistic culture, it remains isolated and cannot be assigned to a genre but only to a text type. However, in Old Testament literature, which is dominated by conventions as compared with modern literature, this eventuality is hardly to be expected. It will almost always be possible to regard a text that at first sight seems isolated as being a transformation of a known genre.

This brings us to the second decisive step in the determination of a genre: this determination is made by comparing our text with texts possessing an analogous organization and intention. The basic means of finding appropriate parallels is a knowledge of the Bible such as is acquired by regular reading of it. A reading of texts related to the specific exegetical work we have in hand, for example, when working on a prophetic text, the reading of the entire book and of thematically similar passages in other prophetic books, will prove helpful in bringing to a successful conclusion the task we have set ourselves. The list of parallels for distinctive phrases and formulas, which we acquired in the work of form criticism, may well provide a comparable service at this point.

The beginner must, of course, be directed to the information available in introductions, monographs, and commentaries, since these, in addition to the academic instruction provided by lectures and seminars, will give him the knowledge he needs of the genres and their terminology. Contrary to an opinion that is widespread today, an eye for the adequacy of exegetical approaches and solutions and an ability to proceed independently in regard to them are not to be gained through private study alone nor even by means of seminars alone. In this area, there can hardly be any substitute for the special function of lectures.

I cannot give a description here of the genres represented in the Old Testament, nor can I involve myself in a discussion of the appropriateness of the more or less accepted *names for the genres*. The former would mean repeating whole pages of books devoted to this subject. The latter would require a special study that includes a survey both of the history of scholarship and of the state of contemporary linguistic and literary studies.

It is clear that at the present time the nomenclature shows a mingling of functional and sociological viewpoints, viewpoints based on the psychology and sociology of literature, and historical viewpoints. Perhaps this is inevitable in the interests of a practicable terminology. It is the role of scholars constantly to be testing the terminology and substituting more appropriate names for those that seem unsuited to the Old Testament material and have perhaps been borrowed from other areas of literary scholarship or from folklore studies. I believe, however, that in their critique scholars should pay attention to the reality-dimension of the genres, such as is reflected in the names myth, tale (*Märchen*), saga, and fable (*Fabel*).[67] The beginner is to be advised, without qualification, to follow the existing nomenclature, to give reasons for his choice if there is a divergence in nomenclature, and in any case to avoid neologisms of his own.

In this context, the question must still be asked of how the determinination of the *Sitz im Leben* of a text is concretely to be accomplished. In dealing with spacious narratives of the kind we associate with history, short story, or novel, such as we have the story of the succession to the throne of David,[68] or the novella about Joseph, or the books of Jonah, Ruth, and Esther, and in the Old Testament books generally, we can make the point, first of all, that they are located within a literature. But a question then immediately arises: What is the *Sitz im Leben* of this literature itself, that is, for what circle of readers was it intended and, if occasion arose, for what public or semipublic reading of it, and where and by whom? In light of a passage like Deuteronomy 31:9ff. and of rabbinic and synagogal practice, we will answer this question by pointing to the readings conducted in the context of the liturgy. On the other hand, Deuteronomy 17:18–19 and Hosea 1:2 also force us to take into account private reading by the believer. Insofar as a group of educated people existed in Israel, we must figure that they would be in mind, from the outset, as readers of the story of the succession to the throne, the other historical narratives, the collections of proverbs, and the sapiential teachings.[69]

I begin with these considerations in order to show that the question of the *Sitz im Leben* can be answered not only in relation to individual texts but also at each higher level and, more frequently than the relevant literature would lead us to think, especially at the next higher literary level, for example, an entire stratum that has been reworked.

In the case of an individual text, the context allows us to infer a group of addressees, specified or unspecified. We may regard the addressees as unspecified when the text does not primarily serve any local interest or instrumental purpose, or else such interests are evidently pushed into the background in favor of an expressly envisaged total Israel, or all of Israel can be provisionally assumed to be the addressee. The addressees are specified when the interests and concerns of certain groups of persons, classes of persons, or individuals are the focus of attention or may be provisionally assumed to be the focus.

In both cases, this means that there is question of a fundamental or perhaps just a special life-situation. The specification of addressees is thus derived either from explicit indications of who they are or, more frequently, from inferences based on content.

In a similar manner, we ascertain the group that the possible author represents by determining the competence or qualifications objectively presupposed by what he says. Such a determination supposes a knowledge of historical institutions and basic situations, both individual and collective, as seen in their transformations within the concrete course of history with its religious, political, and social aspects. At the same time, this knowledge is supplemented and corrected by the results of the investigation.[70]

I may illustrate what has been said by giving two examples. The sacrificial ritual in Leviticus 1–7 is primarily addressed to a group of individuals who are responsible for the observance of the ritual, namely, the priests. As far as authorship is concerned, it is again to the priesthood that we look first of all because of the qualifications they have. If we consider the diachronic aspect, the problem of the text's prehistory in terms of oral or written tradition arises,[71] since it cannot be simply assumed without qualification that sacrifice had been a priestly privilege in the preexilic period; compare, for example, Genesis 12:8, Judges 6:19ff., 2 Samuel 6:17, 1 Kings 8:62–63, and Job 1:5, with, for example, Deuteronomy 12:5ff., Genesis 9:2ff., 2 Chronicles 7:4ff., 23:18, and 26:18. From this, it is clear that a necessary first step is to clarify the stratification of the text by means of literary criticism and then, as circumstances require, by means of genre criticism of a higher order to relate the ritual regulations in the basic stratum to the still more original basic forms[72] that have been reworked.[73] Various considerations show that as far as its date is concerned the text probably belongs to an advanced stage in the formation of the tradition, but that a more exact dating is possible only by combining an investigation and evaluation of the sacrificial torah as a whole with the situation of this last in the context of its literary stratum in the Pentateuch and of the history of institutions (in this case, the priesthood).[74]

On the other hand, the passage in Deuteronomy 4:1–8,[75] which we may here regard as a unit, is expressly addressed to Israel, which means primarily to the male population who are capable of taking part in the cultus. The instruction given evidently supposes that a qualified set of authors must be looked for in a group whose interests and qualifications transcend the purely cultic. The parenetic character of the passage lifts it above both the ritual and the nomistic styles. We must therefore assume either that in the course of time the priestly class came to regard itself as preserver of the entire sacral and religious tradition of the people or else that another group, perhaps the Levites (cf. Deut 31:9), who were the precursor of the later scribal class, is speaking here. The answer to this question clearly requires the literary criticism and tradition criticism of the entire book. The mingling of legal, cultic, and sapiential terminology and the purely religious appraisal given in verses 6–8 of Israel's position in the pagan world lead us to conjecture that in relative terms the text situates us at an advanced or even a late stage in the formation of the tradition, whereas in absolute terms it takes us into the period after the loss of independent statehood and at least into the time when Judaism is being newly consolidated as a religious community. The text is thus an example of the overlapping interplay of various approaches to the determination of a *Sitz im Leben;* it reminds us once again that this problem can often be solved only after working through an entire book.

In addition, the two examples show how the response to the question of the *Sitz im Leben* provides a bridge between genre study as a systematic and classificatory science and genre history as a historical science.

The largely, and inevitably, hypothetical character of the response to the question of the *Sitz im Leben,* and the consequences this response may have in reconstructing the history of tradition and the history of institutions, are a warning against letting imagination have free rein in this area. Nothing is a greater disservice to scientific knowledge than to allow an undisciplined superstructure to be built on the base of an approach that in and of itself is sound. All efforts to situate a text, as well as all the constructions and conclusions, both retrospective and prospective, in the areas of literary history, genre history, and tradition history, that are regarded as implicit in this situation, must be subjected to the test of whether and to what extent they can be concretely located in the life of Israel and Judaism as this is known to us from other sources.[76]

VI   Particular Forms of Exegesis: Interpretation of Words and Subject Matters

Various approaches: semantics, history of oral and written traditions, history of religion, history, and specific subject matters

The *particular forms of exegesis* serve to give material underpinning to the subject context exegesis (*Zusammen-hangsexegese*) in which all the steps in the exegetical process are taken and integrated into total interpretation. The first thing to be done with any text is to determine the meaning, synchronic and diachronic, of the words that contribute to an understanding of the text. I am referring to the kind of thing that is done for every language in a concrete *semantics* or semasiology as science of the meaning of words.[77] On the one hand, the results of such a semantics are entered in general lexicons.[78] On the other, the way is prepared and the results actually arrived at in special dictionaries.[79]

In determining the *meaning of a word,* we begin with the fact that of itself the word has a definite sense but that within each context it acquires a more particular meaning. In the history of a language, *changes of meaning* take place as the result of linguistic conservatism and linguistic innovations, such as the transfer of names due to similarities and contiguities of sense and transfers of sense due to similarities and contiguities of names to a change of meaning through several stages. As a result of these changes of meaning, words acquire a polyvalence that is ascertained in its diachronic historical aspect by means of historical longitudinal sections and synchronic cross-sections.[80]

In work on a particular text, proper procedure requires us to find the range of meanings with the help of the lexicons and then to determine the meaning that fits the context. The general or specific meaning that the lexicons may assign to this passage as one example of the word's use must in every case be tested by comparison with the context and in the light of parallel and divergent meanings of the word. Among the aids used, the concordance comes first[81]; second place belongs to any special studies in periodicals and monographs,[82] these being discovered with the help of the lexicons and a bibliography.[83] As at previous stages of the exegetical process, use is now made of secondary literature only when the interpreter has worked out a meaning for himself, even if this be quite provisional.

The student will turn first to parallels within the same source or primary text or stratum; then he will turn to approximately contemporary literature, earlier literature, and later literature, in that order. As circumstances dictate, he will look not only to parallel concepts, be they similar or contrary, but also to their roots in a specific genre. Here special attention must be paid to the nuances that one and the same concept may have due to its links with various genres. The study of the history of concepts and the study of the history of the written tradition go hand in hand here, in order to determine as accurately as possible the meaning a word has in the text being studied. But the knowledge gained by historical investigation should not lead the interpreter to overlook the decisive function of the immediate context in determining meaning.

With regard to the problem of special theological meanings for Old Testament words, we must observe, with James Barr, that in dealing with the Old Testament we may not in principle suppose any extensive specialization of vocabulary, since in Israel the religious, national, and linguistic communities were identical and did not experience the separation between religious community and everyday linguistic environment that we find in, for example, Alexandrian Judaism.[84] Theological usage and the meaning words had in everyday usage were to a large extent directly connected, within the framework of the differentiations supplied by the everyday language. We may assume a special application of terms (an application that is in any case a matter more of emotional overtone than of semantically definable meaning) only when a word became an element in a specifically theological motif and, as such, was known by its users to have this meaning only in a special context, or when it described some special place or object that was sacral in the narrow sense. Obviously, I am not saying that there were no special technical terms in the language of law, cultus, and ritual.

In a diachronic study of linguistic usage, we are often already dealing in fact with the place of the text in the history of literary tradition. Perhaps German Old Testament scholars, like others, should make a clear distinction between oral tradition (*Überlieferung* and written or literary tradition (*Tradition*) as names for two processes of transmitting material or for the end results of these processes.[85] On the other hand, we must, for the sake of clarity, determine from the context which type of transmission or which type of material or subject matter we are discussing. Here we may define material or subject matter (*Stoff*) as "that which exists and is transmitted apart from any literary work [or: text[86]] and now provides the latter's content."[87]

In the case of both oral and written tradition, part of the subject matter is a class of persons whose functions are to be ascertained and who may be connected with institutions. Their identity may be learned by a process analogous to that applied in determining the speaker or author in connection with the specification of the *Sitz im Leben*.[88]

We may assume the presence of an *oral tradition* when a text or group of texts manifests tensions or stratifications between the basic text and the parts or elements of the framework, yet no written original can be evidenced or be even shown to have probably existed.[89] An oral tradition is also to be assumed when a theme, subject matter, or motif cannot be shown, with certainty or probability, to have been invented and when no intermediate literary stage can be shown to have existed between the literary end-result and the probable original *Sitz im Leben*. The introduction of probability as a criterion shows the hypothetical character of any identification of an oral tradition and of the entire construction of any history of written tradition, necessary though such a construction is for dealing with the content. This kind of construction provides the best, although not the only, means of reconstructing the prehistory and early history of Israel.[90]

In any event, this approach, which was established by Hermann Gunkel and variously developed in Scandinavia by Sigmund Mowinckel[91] and Ivan Engnell and the Uppsala School[92] and in Germany especially under the influence of Albrecht Alt and his disciples, is now a part of our science. It must, however, by applied with special methodological caution and self-criticism.[93]

The probelm of the history of literary tradition arises when a theme or motif proves to have been transmitted in writing, or when a similar transmission is to be supposed for reasons having to do with a specific subject matter, as, for example, in the case of a list that has been inserted into a narrative and is judged by historical criticism to be a primary document. In the last analysis, the whole matter of literary dependencies and borrowings falls under the history of written or literary tradition. In Germany, the *history of literary tradition* is often not distinguished clearly from the history of oral tradition, and in fact the two can often be objectively distinguished only with great difficulty. However, during the first two decades after the Second World War, the history of literary tradition became central to the study of sapiential, juridical, cultic, and prophetic literature. The results of this history, along with the results of work on the history of oral tradition, have been subjected to a (still incomplete) checking and modification[94] as the result of new attention given to the history of religions[95] and to literary criticism and of the discovery of redaction criticism and redaction history.[96] The results of a consistent implementation of a program for genre history, the history of oral and written tradition, and redaction history play a part in tracing the history of the canon.[97]

Given the predominantly religious nature of the material, any work on the history of written and oral tradition must be closely connected with the *history of Old Testament religion*.[98] It also leads beyond the latter into the field of the history of religion in *Canaan and Syria,* Egypt, Asia Minor, and Mesopotamia, especially when it focuses on the history of individual genres, institutions, and ideas and thus shows how relevant the religious history of these geographical areas is. Attention to the relevant literatures has already played a role in the discussion of genre history.[99] It is obvious that all the objects and vital expressions of alien religions that are mentioned in the text being investigated call for careful clarification. In the process, the present contribution that they may make to the concrete exegetical task is certainly to be kept in view, but on the other hand this approach should not be robbed of its value by being conceived in too narrow a manner. Thus, when one must for solid reasons reckon with borrowings or wishes to understand the positions represented by the texts, one must acquire a clear understanding of the value and function of the phenomena in their original as well their present religious context and not too hastily eliminate the individuality of religious manifestations by the application of phenomenology or of an untested hypothesis about a "pattern" or religious structural model that fits the entire ancient Near East, Israel included.[100] I do not mean to deny the legitimacy of approaches that are based on a phenomenology of religion and that focus attention on the common elements (which are based on universal human nature) in religious attitudes, actions, and institutions (these last resulting from the fact that being-in-the-world is a constitutive aspect of the human person).[101] But the exegete must be aware (nor, as a theologian, may he never forget) that religion is always found in a concrete form and in a concrete community.[102]

In our reflections on the exegesis of specific subject matter, we return almost to our starting point, the investigation of details, when we recall that all personal names must be explained as such; that their owners must be identified as far as possible; that all supposedly historical occurrences must be verified, all place names and other geographical details must be identified, and all cultural objects and practices must be ascertained. The *semantics of names,*[103] historical *prosopography,*[104] the *history of Israel* in the context of the *history of ancient Near Eastern peoples and cultures,*[105] the *historical geography*[106] and *regional geography of Palestine,*[107] the *study of antiquity* that reconstructs life as lived in biblical times,[108] and the *archeology* of Syria and Palestine:[109] all these with their findings will make their contribution here. Finally, we may not overlook *biblical anthropology.*[110]

The brevity of the present essay does not permit me to discuss the particular methods of these various disciplines. However, given the special importance of the historical approach for the entire interpretation, I must at least mention the general *criteria* used in judging the *historical value* of the information in a *historical source*. First, the historian must determine the source's *relation to reality* (*Wirklichkeitshorizont*). Evidently, the *literary character* of the source—a saga, a legend, a chronicler's notice giving fictitious causes of an event, an annalistic notice, annals, a story, a letter, a treaty, or a piece of critical historical description—indicates in each case a different kind of relation to reality. To this divergence corresponds in turn a different selection of material from the historical continuum and a specific intention or purpose that the historian must ascertain before he can evaluate the source. For example, one must know the stylistic laws and principles of selection proper to an Egyptian or a Mesopotamian royal inscription if proper use is to be made of the inscription in the investigation of historical events.

Second, the historian must show a factual or conceivable continuity of testimony between the event reported or referred to and its first and subsequent literary attestations down to the source with which the historian is now dealing. Third, the historian must apply the *general criteria of probability or evidence*.[111]

In the course of our exegetical work, we have already made a general determination of the horizon of reality in connection with the determination of genre; now, in the examination of concrete content, we must draw the conclusions from that earlier decision.[112] This will prevent our approaching the text in inappropriate and subjective ways, such as would result, for example, from mistaking a story for an historical account. The theologian may repeat Hamlet's famous remark, but he must also ask himself honestly whether he is giving the spirit priority over the letter and whether his caution (often quite appropriate) springs from fear of God as Lord of reality or rather from an unacknowledged fear on behalf of God! In the interests, then, of the greatest possible objectivity, the determination of the genre and of its specific relation to reality must play a very decisive role in historical criticism. The ascertainment of the author's purpose points the way to the ascertainment of the intention of the text, which is turn is part of the subsequent continuous exposition (*Gesamtinterpretation*).[113]

VII Remarks on the Continuous Exposition of the Text

Now that all the preliminary stages thus far described have been completed (or, more accurately, now that the viewpoints important for these stages have been described), we clear our work table and will do well to put the job aside for a few days, in order to acquire the necessary distance from our detailed work and thus to achieve the comprehensive grasp that is required for a unified presentation of our results. We might well use these intervening days to give the necessary finishing touches to the *translation*. If throughout the entire exegetical process we have kept our eye on the rough translation we made at the beginning and have corrected it as we advanced, all that will be needed now is a little polishing.

The beginner may regard the translation as the simplest thing of all, but in fact it is the most difficult part of the exegete's work. Translation is a demanding art that calls for the gift of empathy in regard to the foreign language no less than for a mastery of one's own. A scientific translation endeavors to travel the narrow path between two precipices: on the one side, a slavish and, when possible, etymologically determined transposition that imitates the sentence structure and style of the original text, and, on the other, a transfer that makes free use of the equivalences and stylistic devices of both languages for the purpose of a maximal adaptation of the text to the language of the contemporary world. In the process, the translator must be careful about the suitability of language to object and avoid using a mechanical, commonplace vocabulary for highly stylized sacral texts or an artificially refined jargon for unpretentiously simple stories or tired clichés from everyday life for prophetic oracles that are freighted with meaning. Consistency in choosing equivalents can be a necessary virtue or can make the translation ludicrous.[114]

During our recess from work on the text, we must consider, first, whether we want to conduct the continuous exposition of the text (usually called *context exegesis*) under a single comprehensive viewpoint or under several varying viewpoints that approximately correspond to the stages of the exegetical process; and, second, which approach we shall use in beginning this exposition. If the presentation is being made in the framework of scientific discussion, the proper thing is to take the state of the discussion as our point of departure and to give prominence to points of view that have been undervalued or given insufficient attention, with the result that the problems have not received an adequate solution.

If the exposition is not being addressed to specific professional readership, it may be preferable to focus on a problem that our contemporaries find intelligible and existentially important. But care must be taken not to allow any qualitative impoverishment of the material when thus shifting from a historical to a hermeneutic perspective. We may be addressing the reader of a higher level, but this does not justify scanting the exegete's work. In one manner or another we must inform the reader about the literary character of the text, its unity and genre, its age and place of origin, the author(s) or mediating agents, the addressees, the situation that is presupposed, the intention behind the statements and the stylistic devices that serve this intention, the material contents and their relation to historical reality, and the religious and theological content as seen against the background of its historical context and accompanied by an exposition of any abiding elements that reveal fundamental possibilities of human existence.

Finally, we must decide whether we will proceed verse by verse or rather give an interpretation that is structured by the problems to be solved. It may be that a text, in a positive or a negative way, forces us to ask whether and in what respect it is of any concern to us after so long a time. We should not drag this question in by force, but neither should we timidly avoid it. In this regard, we must note very carefully whether the text really requires to be considered from a religious or theological viewpoint. If circumstances call for it, we must not hesitate to characterize secular or pseudo-religious intentions as what they in fact are, but on the other hand we must make such a judgment in terms of the text's own understanding of reality or expressly call attention to the difference between its understanding of reality and our understanding of it today, lest we be found guilty of indulging in unhistorical and therefore inappropriate judgments. There are also texts whose contents are incomprehensible to us today or which, apart from their value in helping us to reconstruct the human universe of that time, are, for the present and perhaps permanently, simply museum pieces.

As attorney for a text whose author can no longer defend or explain himself, we must exhaust all possibilities for understanding it before we declare it to incomprehensible. As attorney for the present age in confrontation with the text, we must exhaust all possibilities for explaining it before we allow it to cast doubt on our understanding of reality. Faith in God is an exception to such doubt, to the extent that faith is the presupposition and premise of our self-understanding and, in any event, cannot be acquired by induction. But the privilege does not extend to the concepts that interpret our faith in a language and form derived from the world. The cause of religion and thus of the human beings and human society in whose name we do our work is always better served by straightforward candor than by an affected profundity and a bigotry that closes its eyes to reality. But even where honesty reigns, there is an abiding difference between reality as seen through the eyes of faith and hope and reality as seen without faith and hope; the difference is one that makes itself felt not in the way we address ourselves to details but in the character of our whole outlook and mentality.

There are two further questions; the first is whether we are explicitly to relate our Old Testament text to the New Testament message, along the lines of biblical theology and with consideration given to the transformations that have taken place in the history of the Church as well as to what has been called the "transformation of Christian thinking in modern times"[115]; the second is whether we are in like manner to situate the Old Testament text within the horizon of contemporary faith and life. The answer to the questions will depend on the character of the text, on the purpose of our work, and, when the results of this are in, on our concrete ideas regarding faith.

If we are properly to exercise the two functions of attorney for the text in relation to the present age and attorney for the present age in relation to the text, we must separate the two functions as clearly as possible in the presentation of our work. It must be clear at every point which role we are adopting, which presupposition lies behind our argument. Since our particular piece of work is only one item within the overarching world of scientific scholarship, we can adopt a much more modest goal than the hermeneutic re-presentation of the Old Testament text, our work being meant, for example, as a contribution to the solution of an unresolved problem in literary history or the history of religions or secular history. The exegete may not, of course, simply assume that others will accept the hermeneutic task. It is only for a time that he can restrict himself to the function—which is admittedly his first obligation—of being attorney for the text before the present age. This image of an attorney (if I may stay with it for a moment) makes it clear once again that the distinction between the historical task and the hermeneutic task can only be a matter of emphasis, for an attorney must speak in a way that is clear and understandable to judge, jury, and public alike.[116]

The horizon chosen and the importance of the results sought in the investigation will determine the style and breadth of our presentation. Scholarship requires that we give reasons for our judgments and avoid unfounded assertions; that we make clear our dependence on the work of others; that we specify the degree of probability of our results; that we present unsettled or presently insoluble or newly arisen problems for what they are and, if circumstances permit, give the reasons why we have not gone into them or given answers. Language that is simple and to the point and sentences that are clearly structured are preferable to bombast and pedantry. Accuracy and the verifiable clarity and reliability of our information and assertions will determine the scientific value of our work.

Werner Georg Kümmel

✤　✤　✤

NEW TESTAMENT EXEGESIS

The Point of View in Exegesis

Anyone who is interested in the exegesis of a New Testament text must be clear in his own mind about what it is that he wants to achieve. One can, in principle, approach the New Testament just as one can approach any other written tradition, from various perspectives: "an interpretation is . . . always oriented toward a specific way of asking questions, toward a specific point of view."[1] In the context of this introduction, it is true, we shall take for granted that a number of the possible ways of raising questions that are in themselves important are, as a rule, of no interest to the beginner or have significance only for specialists (e.g., the questions raised by specialists in grammar, historical linguistics, or the history of ideas). On the other hand, even a beginner who has no such specialized interests must keep clearly in mind which of the two obvious ways of asking questions he will use in dealing with a particular exegetical problem, inasmuch as the following two ways of approaching a problem may be adopted as easily by the theological student as by the advanced exegete, especially in regard to the New Testament:

a] I intend, by scientific exegesis, to learn from the text what it says about the historical circumstances at the time of its composition, about its author and the readers for whom it was intended, about the intellectual milieu from which it

43

originates, about the external or internal history of primitive Christianity, etc.

b] I intend, by scientific exegesis, to discover the objective meaning of the text, that is, to learn from the text what it says about the subject matter discussed in it, and what this means for me personally.

These two approaches are equally legitimate, and the historical point of view is certainly not admissible only for historians and philologists. Work on the history of primitive Christianity, on the biography of Paul, on questions about the origin and interrelationship of the New Testament scriptures, etc., is also indispensable for the theologian, for the understanding of primitive Christianity and the individual New Testament books. This point must be emphasized, however, because the recognition of the fundamental justification of *both* approaches must not be wrongly understood to imply that questions about the subject matter of a text can be answered *directly*. It is essential, rather, for all students engaged in exegetical work on the New Testament to understand that questions about the subject matter of a New Testament text can be answered only by way of a historical investigation of the text. Even if I do not mean to inquire explicitly about the grammar or about the historical and religious background of a passage under consideration, I cannot evade questions from these points of view if I wish to answer questions about the subject matter of the text reliably. The meaning of the subject matter of the text and, therefore, its meaning for me can open up for me only if I have understood what the text was intended to say, in accordance with the purpose of its author, to the readers he first had in view—in his and their language. Every kind of subject exegesis is an interpretation of the text itself, and not an arbitrary violation of the text, only if it attempts to bring the historical meaning of the text, in its historical context, to new life. For, of itself, the ancient text is mute, and only by scientific scholarly effort can it be made to speak again, at least in some measure.

I Text of the New Testament: Textual Criticism

To facilitate the discussion of further methodological procedures, I shall assume from now on that the question the student means to put to the text is, generally speaking, that which is concerned with the meaning of the subject matter of the text. In view of the nature of the New Testament scriptures, which we have briefly indicated above, this question can be answered only by moving step by step toward the recovery of the original meaning of a text. Presupposed for this gradual recovery of the meaning of a text is, of course, the knowledge of the text itself, in its original wording.

The fact that we have at our disposal, in E. Nestle's and K. Aland's edition of the Greek New Testament,[2] a reliable and widely recognized "average text" must not lead us to the mistaken conclusion that the Nestle text can be accepted as the original text without further ado. Rather, the student must be clear on two points: (1) The text of Nestle's edition is a mechanically produced average text based on the scholarly editions in use at the end of the nineteenth century. Even though this mechanically created text has recently been altered in a few places (e.g., in John 1:21) contrary to this principle, it does not always by any means reflect the critical opinions of its editors. The Nestle text is not intended to be correct in *every* place. (2) To make proper use of the Nestle text, one must re-examine the critical apparatus again and again, and hence the beginner must, as soon as possible, with the help of the introduction to the Nestle edition, acquire a knowledge of the symbols and most important manuscript abbreviations employed in textual criticism. Indeed, the ability to read the apparatus is still not sufficient to enable one to judge the value of the attestation of a variant reading; for this, one must know something of the history of the text and some of the most important rules for deciding questions of textual criticism. Whoever is unable to become acquainted with the fundamentals of New Testament textual criticism from lectures on the subject or from practical training in it should, therefore, as soon as possible, work carefully through a short exposition of the subject.[3]

The knowledge of textual criticism gained in this way can, to be sure, be applied only in connection with exegesis itself, and it is quite inexpedient to try to establish a text from the point of view of textual criticism at the start, independently of exegesis, though this is exactly what beginners like to do. It is therefore recommended that the student school his judgment in the use of textual criticism, while engaged in exegesis, by thinking through each decision for or against variants offered in the apparatus even if they are not essential for understanding the text (no example of such variants can be considered in what follows).

II Linguistic Resources

The second indispensable step in recovering the original meaning of a text is to strive for a *linguistic* understanding, i.e., for a correct translation of the text. A knowledge of the vocabulary is not enough to enable one to translate the text, though this is naturally presupposed. Whoever wishes to translate a New Testament text that is not at first completely intelligible (e.g., Mark 15:26) must be informed about the *various possible meanings* of the ambiguous words and about the *grammatical possibilities* in the constructions involved. From this, it is clear that for working out a correct translation both a dictionary and a grammar are indispensable. Since the Greek used by the authors of the New Testament is no longer the classical language but a variety of Hellenistic Greek, one must always take account of the possibility that a change may have taken place in the use of a word or of a grammatical construction in the passage from classical to Hellenistic Greek. Furthermore, if the student is to be aware of such changes and be informed about the range of possible meanings for a word, he must make a survey of the occurrences of the word in its different meanings as well as of the various translations that have been proposed; for this reason he should avoid using school dictionaries, pocket dictionaries, "keys," and the like, all of which may be very useful in their proper place.

A comprehensive view of the whole of classical and Hellenistic Greek usage is furnished in the dictionary of Liddell and Scott, but such exhaustive information is normally unnecessary, and the dictionary that suffices for all ordinary purposes is that of Bauer, Arndt, and Gingrich (this the student should own, if possible).[4] The beginner should make it a rule to look up in the latter all words whose meaning is not completely unambiguous and, circumstances permitting, should work through the other passages cited there and the bibliographical references as well, insofar as it seems useful to do so (looking up the references given there to parallels in the Apostolic Fathers or in early Jewish or secular literature can be very helpful in many cases). Similarly, grammatical questions that arise in translating, especially those dealing with syntax, cannot be fully answered with the help of an introductory grammar alone. The best resource here, which should be consulted rather than read, is the *Grammar of the Greek New Testament,* by F. Blass and A. Debrunner, translated by R. Funk. The revision of the German original by F. Rehkopf (1976[14]) is much easier to use than the preceding recent editions with their Supplement; but references to the earlier editions are easily followed up since the numbering of the paragraphs remains unchanged. A short book by C. F. D. Moule is also very instructive, and may be read with profit.[5] With these resources, one can work out a provisional translation, which must, of course, be confirmed by the appropriate exegetical considerations. Indeed, modern scholarly translations (in commentaries or separately published[6]) may serve as controls for one's own translation, but to use these before ne has completed one's own exegesis is strongly to be discouraged, since otherwise it is easy for one to neglect to make the sentence structure and the different possibilities for translating the text really clearly to oneself, and far too easy for one to fail to see how uncertain one or another proposed translation may be.

III   Questions of Introduction

If one wishes to understand a text in its original sense, one must also be acquainted with the circumstances in which the writing in which the text appears came into being. This information can be obtained only by investigating the writing itself together with all other evidence about the writing and its author. But, desirable as it may be for the student to pursue such an investigation as an individual project in the course of his study, perhaps in a seminar report, it is impossible to carry out such an investigation by oneself in every case; hence, in general, as a further preparatory step in interpreting a New Testament text, one turns to the appropriate scholarly literature for information on the so-called "questions of introduction" that concern the writing under consideration.

Here there are three possibilities: (1) A student may read the introduction to a scientific commentary on the writing concerned. It should be noted, however, that only the more *comprehensive* introductions are adequate for this purpose (hence, perhaps, not those in *Das Neue Testament Deutsch*), that not all commentaries have introductions that deal with these questions, and that the introductions in older commentaries can no longer serve this purpose, even if their exegesis still retains its value. (2) One may read the articles dealing with the writing in question in the major reference works (RGG, LThK, etc.), which are frequently very comprehensive and have good bibliographies; however, these articles do not undertake in all cases to survey the historical problems. (3) One may read the appropriate section in a standard "Introduction to the New Testament" textbook[7] and, if necessary, look up particular details in the specialized works mentioned in the bibliographies given there. Here it is important, not so much to be informed about all the problems presented by the New Testament book in question, as to be clear about the historical context and prehistory of the text to be interpreted. However, it is especially important to keep clearly in mind what can and what cannot be known with certainty, so that the exposition of the text is not based on mere suppositions as if they were assured results.

IV   The Task of Exegesis

After the student has completed this preliminary general survey of the manuscript tradition, the problems of translation, and the historical uncertainties surrounding a text, he can proceed with the exegesis proper. This is the point at which a clear and careful answer must be given to the question mentioned at the outset: What do I want to achieve by my exegesis? For it is the aim that I have in view that will determine whether I concentrate my interest primarily on questions about the origin and historical content of a writing, on questions about its wider religious context and background, on biographical or more strictly historical questions, or on religious and properly theological questions. For considerations of space, we shall confine ourselves to the single aim of searching out and interpreting the objective meaning of the text, and thereby also of gaining insight into the theological problems touched on in the text. Similar methodological considerations apply when the exegesis has other ends in view.

When we undertake to discover the objective meaning of a New Testament passage, it is methodologically essential for us to differentiate between the Synoptic Gospels, on the one hand, and the remaining New Testament books, on the other.

a] For the majority of the New Testament books, the essential task consists in investigating the meaning of the statements of the author of the writing in question and in setting the statements of individual passages in their context in the writing or corpus of writings concerned. Where we know that a literary relationship exists between texts we are studying (e.g., between Colossians and Ephesians, or Jude and 2 Peter), the consideration of this relationship can help us in our interpretation of the dependent writing only in that it enables us better to understand the special characteristics of a passage as it deviates from the original.

b] It is otherwise with the Synoptics. Here, three or four steps are methodologically necessary if we wish to grasp the meaning of a text completely, particularly where Jesus' words, or stories about Jesus, are present (not, perhaps, for passages peculiar to the different evangelists, e.g., Luke 1:1–4 or Matthew 28:16–20).

1. First, we are confronted by the text in context as formulated by the evangelist, and we have to ask ourselves what the evangelist means to say in a particular passage in the context of his Gospel. That is, questions about the wording, the correct translation, etc. naturally arise first vis-à-vis the Gospel as it lies before us, or as it can be established by textual criticism.

2. Even when the explanation of a Synoptic passage in the context of the Gospel concerned does not lead to questions incapable of being answered on the basis of *this* context, we cannot, when dealing with Matthew and Luke, leave out of account the fact that they have a large part of their subject matter in common with Mark and a further part in common with each other. To be sure, the solution of the Synoptic Problem is still not entirely settled, but it is just here

that one must be quite clear—at least in theory and in general—about questions of introduction that are relevant for the passage being interpreted, if one wishes to give an adequate interpretation for a Synoptic text. Even if one does not accept the two-source theory, which is presupposed in the following discussion,[8] one must try to explain the literary relationship between the Synoptics somehow, and take account of this explanation in one's exegesis. The second step of the exegetical task here, therefore, is to inquire further about the sources that are extant or that may be conjectured to underlie two Gospels, and that make the form of the text as we have it more or less easy to understand.

In connection with the two approaches just described, the "redaction-history method" made its appearance in Synoptic scholarship after the Second World War and nowadays plays a dominant role in commentaries and especially in monographic literature and in essays on the individual Synoptic Gospels, as well as on particular texts.[9] The question of the special literary and theological intention of each evangelist may not be neglected if one wishes to understand the intention of the statements the evangelist is making in a particular text. And where the original that an evangelist has reworked is known to us or can on good grounds be surmised (as with Matthew and Luke in relation to Mark), such an approach has a relatively secure basis. On the other hand, the redaction-history approach as applied to the Gospel of Mark or to the material peculiar to an individual evangelist must inevitably be based on pure conjecture. For this reason, though it is important for a beginner to take the redaction-history approach into consideration in his interpretation of a Synoptic text, he must at the same time be advised to exercise critical caution if he wishes to avoid the snare of pulling more out of texts than they are saying with certainty.

3. Behind the literary sources that are extant or that may be inferred, however, lies the oral tradition, which took

shape in the believing community. This insight of the form-critical school[10] is generally accepted today, even if widely varying inferences are drawn from it. Exegesis should, however, by no means seek to discover only the theological significance of a tradition in the context of a Gospel, but also to press forward to the form of the tradition as the evangelist himself received it. Furthermore, this form lies either directly behind the text as we received it (as in Mark or in the special sources of Matthew or Luke) or behind the sayings-source (commonly referred to as Q), which may be inferred to underlie parts of Matthew and Luke.

4. Whether it is the task of the exegete to take still another step further back and to ask about the form of the saying on the lips of Jesus or of the account that goes back to the life of Jesus, or to decide *whether* the saying or account does in fact go back to the historical Jesus, is disputed. Whoever (like the author of this essay[11]) gives an affirmative answer here will regard it as the last and decisive part of the task of interpreting a Synoptic text to ask also about the meaning and form of a saying or account in its oldest attainable form, and about its relationship to the proclamation of the Gospel and to the work of Jesus.

V   Resources for Exegesis

Apart from the somewhat different approach required in the study of Synoptic texts, which we have discussed above, exegetical procedure is the same for all texts. The methodological ideal in interpreting a text is to interpret it as a component part of a larger whole; hence, in a measure, interpreting a text involves the interpretation of the whole writing. Although it is very desirable for every student to work through a whole New Testament book exegetically—or, indeed, through more than one—this ideal cannot always be realized in practice. Hence, the two following presuppositions must be strictly observed, even if one intends to work through only a small portion of a book.

a] The beginning and end of a section must be carefully defined (the demarcation of the traditional ecclesiastical "pericopes" is often very questionable!), because an individual sentence or idea can be made intelligible only in relation to its own proximate context.

b] Therefore, the wider context of a section to be interpreted must be kept in view, so that one can recognize the sense of an individual idea within this context and from this can correctly perceive the boundaries of the section in which it occurs. To be sure, one cannot take it for granted that a sentence that has come down to us in a particular context can be recognized as having belonged to that context originally. Even if this is assumed as a working hypothesis, it does not always prove to be true, and where no train of thought or logically intelligible relationship can be seen, the connection should not be forced (cf., for example, the series of sayings in Mark 9:48–50 or a paraenetic text like Romans 12:9–21).

The student cannot undertake the demarcation of a section of the text and the examination of its wider context, however, without referring to commentaries or specialized works. Hence an important prerequisite for beginning the work of exegesis is the selection of suitable exegetical aids. Here the student must be warned against a double error. On the one hand, many beginners are inclined to consult as many commentaries as possible, especially if they are readily accessible in a seminar library, and they will then easily be confused or altogether repelled by the fullness of contradictory opinions. Some beginners, on the other hand, content themselves with a single commentary known or recommended to them as good, and thus they gain no adequate insight into the many-sidedness of the problems that can arise. Although for really scientific work one should make as comprehensive use of the literature as possible, those who are just beginning study of this kind will be well advised to limit themselves to two or three commentaries of different types.

No hard and fast rule can be given for selecting these commentaries. The student should acquaint himself with the important series of commentaries and be well aware of their characteristic peculiarities so that he will know where he can expect to find particular kinds of information; however, all the important commentaries do not belong to any one series, and one must keep oneself informed as to what commentaries are available by referring to the most recent of them and to the newest textbooks on New Testament introduction. The selection one makes for oneself, then, will have to be guided by the professor's recommendations or by more experienced fellow students, or even by one's own tentative browsing. To be sure, one must not think that assistance in exegesis is to be found only in the commentaries on the New Testament book being studied; specialized works or essays frequently contain at least as extensive and helpful exegetical explanations, and one should allow oneself to be led to these special works by the references in recent commentaries, in Bauer-Arndt-Gingrich's *Greek-English Lexicon,* in the *Theological Dictionary of the New Testament,* or in articles in other specialized works of reference.

Whenever the subject matter demands it, one can and must refer to specialized works on exegesis in addition to the commentaries. Generally speaking, the commentaries are adequate to enable one to determine the boundaries of a section of the text and to discover its subdivisions, if any, and also to solve many isolated exegetical problems; however, for a deeper understanding of the more important concepts and their intellectual context, one requires information about the history of ideas and about the more general interrelations of religious and theological thought. For dealing with such questions, the most important and indispensable resource is a *concordance*. While for some kinds of work complete concordances are necessary,[12] for most purposes the abridged concordance of O. Schmoller[13] is sufficient; this book should be in the hands of every theological student. With the help of a concordance, one can make a preliminary survey of the use of a word or word-group within a writing, in writings of a single author, or in the whole New Testament, and from this, one can at once gain important insights. However, if the student wishes to put these insights in their historical context, he must make use of other special works, in particular the *Theological Dictionary of the New Testament*.[14] It must be admitted that the articles in this dictionary vary considerably in comprehensiveness and quality, and one cannot always be sure of finding needed information in it; however, as a rule, the bibliographies subjoined to the individual articles, as well as the index volume, supply further assistance. The student will be well advised not to consult an article of the TDNT only where it touches on a text in which he is interested at the time, but whenever possible to read the whole article, since without information about the historical, religious, and conceptual background of a word or an idea, explanations about a single passage cannot be fully understood. The TDNT gives no information about names or concepts that do not belong to theology or to the history of ideas, so that for information about these one must consult the appropriate technical dictionaries as well as larger general works of reference.[15]

After assembling the necessary information with the help of the resources mentioned above and after surveying the various problems and the possibilities for their solution, the student can now approach a text himself and try his hand at an interpretation. Of course, it is not necessary to follow the *sequence of questions* as they are given in this methodological sketch; how one approaches a text depends on the nature of the text itself. The main thing is for all the questions to be taken into account. Furthermore, at every point where it does not seem possible to reach a more or less certain conclusion, it is important not to conceal the fact that no certain or even arguable decision at all is possible and that, consequently, a not inconsiderable number of New Testament texts provide no really firm basis for the proclamation of the Gospel, much less for the definition of doctrine. The assumption that every text *has* to be preached from is false for two reasons.

First, there are numerous "profane" texts in the New Testament, which contain no kerygma of any kind, and which can be made the basis of an existential address only by artificially allegorizing them or by reducing them to a motto (e.g., Mark 6:19–28; Acts 19:23–40).

Second, there are theologically significant texts that resist all exegetical efforts to interpret them with certainty, and the exegete as well as the preacher should guard against pretending—for himself and for others—to a certainty that cannot be attained (e.g., Romans 11:25–26, 32; John 2:1–11). This warning is not intended to encourage the beginner to break off his exegetical work too soon; however, no one can make proper use of the methodological tool kit of pure exegesis unless he understands its limitations and learns to reserve judgment where no certain conclusions may be drawn.

In the following two sections, the method of exegesis will be illustrated in the treatment of two passages; for neither of these is a complete commentary offered, and the exegetical viewpoint presented is not peculiarly my own, but one that is intentionally designed to serve as a methodological model. It should be taken for granted that the texts discussed here involve still other questions and that there are still other solutions besides the ones mentioned here.

VI   *Interpretation of Romans 5:1–11*

For the interpretation of Romans 5:1–11, I have chosen the commentaries of O. Michel, E. Käsemann, and H. Schlier because in these commentaries we have three differing points of view at our disposal: a traditional philological and theological, a modern historical and theological, and a modern Catholic.[16] As far as this text is concerned, questions of introduction may be taken as settled: the Epistle to the Romans is at all events the latest of the major letters of Paul and was written at the end of his so-called third missionary journey. The original unity of Romans 1–15 is likewise challenged today by only a few isolated authors.[17] We can, therefore, proceed on the assumption that Romans 5:1–11 is to be understood as a component part of the train of thought developed in Romans, chapters 1–15.[18] Most commentators agree that the exposition of the theme of Romans 1:16–17 (the righteousness of God is revealed for those who believe in the Gospel) is concluded with 4:25; some scholars, it is true, understand 5:1–11 as continuing the preceding train of thought, and others feel that no new thought is introduced until 6:1.[19] However, Michel shows convincingly that after the creedlike conclusion in 4:23–25 the train of thought takes a new turn in 5:1; chapters 5–8 deal with the new life from God on the *basis* of the revelation of righteousness in the Gospel. Thus the section 5:1–11 presupposes the exposition in 1:16–4:25, but it also introduces a new development in the thought. The end of the section is also clearly marked: still another thought is introduced in 5:12 (the certainty of the eschatological gift of life and righteousness is surer than the sure expectation of death). Romans 5:1—11 can therefore be considered by itself as a clearly defined section.

A preliminary survey of the section shows that three thoughts follow one another: verses 1–5 speak of peace with God, of the hope of glory, and of the situation of the Christian which is characterized by these; verses 6–8 point to the death of Jesus as the reason for this situation; verses 9–11 connect both of these ideas—through the death of Jesus our eschatological hope of salvation has become a certain hope (cf. Michel). It is important to establish the sequence of the individual ideas and, hence, of the subdivisions of the section to be interpreted, because only in this way can the internal relationships of the interconnected single thoughts be understood and be put to service in exegesis.

The first subsection, verses 1–5, brings together three statements:

[a] having been justified, we have peace with God and access to grace;

[b] hence, we exult in our sufferings on the basis of our hope; and [c] this hope receives its power from the Spirit, which has been given to us. The first statement must be based on what precedes, since it is connected with the preceding material by *oun:* the justification described in 3:21–4:25, which has been given to believers, is the basis for maintaining that *eirēnēn echomen.* This reading of the present Nestle text was, as the symbol ▌ in the apparatus indicates, accepted into the text only since the seventeenth edition, contrary to the mechanical principles on which it is based, because the majority of commentators regard this reading as original. Only a few exegetes still defend the reading *echōmen,* which stood in earlier editions of Nestle.[20]

A decision for one reading rather than another will obviously affect the *sense* of the passage quite materially, so that the first business of the interpreter here is to make this textual decision. A glance at the apparatus in the Nestle–Aland edition and in the *Greek New Testament* shows that the subjunctive is substantially better attested; except for later corrections of *Codex Vaticanus* and *Codex Sinaiticus* and for the later majuscule P and a few minuscules, all of which are unimportant from the standpoint of textual criticism, the indicative is probably to be found only, on the one hand, in a fragment of the fourth century (0220), in the late majuscule Ψ and in the Sahidic version (these are all witnesses to the so-called ''Egyptian'' text) and, on the other, in the late majuscule G (*Codex Boernerianus*), which belongs to the so-called ''Western'' text, and perhaps in a late Latin manuscript. This reading is thus lacking in almost all the best witnesses of both the ''Egyptian'' and the ''Western'' texts. Therefore, according to the rules of textual criticism, the subjunctive would have to be regarded as original (it is better attested, since it is found in the generally preferable ''Egyptian'' text and also in most witnesses to the ''Western'' text).

However, if one tries to interpret this reading, it must be understood as an exhortation to maintain (or establish?) peace with God through the mediation of Jesus Christ. Thus it is already unclear what *echōmen* really means in this instance, and such an exhortation does not fit in at all well with the continuation in verse 2, which describes the access to God's grace as a gift that has been received. An examination of the immediate context takes us no further. However, the weakly attested variant *echomen* is still an ancient one (even Codex G reflects an older text), so that possibility of its correctness should be tested by an examination of Paul's use of *eirēnē*.

Since the three commentaries we are using do not help us here (but cf. Schlier),[21] we turn to Schmoller's concordance.[22] Here we find that Paul can indeed use *eirēnē* of the relation of human beings to one another, but that where *eirēnē* describes the relation of mankind to God, God appears as the originator of *eirēnē*. For confirmation of this survey of Pauline linguistic usage, we refer to the article on *eirēnē* in TDNT (II, 415; W. Foerster), where it is pointed out that a few verses further on, in Romans 5:10, it is said that men were enemies of God and that God reconciled them to himself through the death of his Son. Thus, it should be clear that the weakly attested reading *echomen,* in spite of its weak attestation, must be correct (and we can learn from Käsemann and Foerster how the early origin of the incorrect reading can perhaps be explained).

Still another textual decision must be made before we can translate verses 1–2 with assurance: Do the words *tēi pistei,* which are bracketed in Nestle's text, belong in the text or not? Here again, the commentaries disagree. Käsemann sends us to Lietzmann's older commentary for the reasons for regarding these words as original, and they are also very well attested, but it is difficult to decide the question with certainty.[23] However, it is not of great importance for the exegesis, because the role of faith in man's reception of righteousness has already been emphasized in verse 1. In any event, these two textual problems that we have briefly considered here will help to make clear to the beginner that, in spite of all the progress that has been made in textual criticism, there are still many variants that are fundamental for an *objective* understanding of individual texts, and yet that cannot be accepted or rejected with complete certainty.

After these preliminary textual questions have been settled, the translation of verses 1–2 offers no special difficulty. Nonetheless, Käsemann warns us at verse 2 against pressing the *kai* before *tēn prosagōgēn,* and thus makes us aware of a logical difficulty presented by the usual translation, "through whom we have access" (Michel, Schlier): the grace in which Christians stand has not been made accessible to them by Christ *among others.* If we turn to Bauer–Arndt–Gingrich's *Lexicon* for light on this difficulty, we find under *kai,* II, 6, the information that *kai,* in combination with the relative pronoun, lends greater independence to the following relative clause (Romans 9:24 is adduced, correctly, to substantiate this point). We should, therefore, probably not translate the *kai* in Romans 5:2 at all, or, possibly, render it by "indeed."[24] Paul thus infers from the gift of righteousness that is experienced in faith that, through Christ, peace with God is established for Christians and access to this grace is created as a reality of the existence of those who believe.[25]

This statement is now qualified by verses 2b–5. With a simple *kai,* which conceals for the moment the logic of his thought, Paul adds: *kauchōmetha ep' elpidi tēs doxēs tou theou,* and follows this with another *kauchōmetha,* introduced by a favorite elliptical phrase, *ou monon de.* A glance at the concordance shows at once that Paul frequently (as in verse 3) attaches the object or cause of boasting to *kauchasthai* with *en.* The combination of *kauchasthai* with *epi* (as in verse 2b), on the other hand, is not found elsewhere in Paul (nor, for that matter, in the whole New Testament). Bauer's *Lexicon* tells us, however, that this combination does occur in profane Greek as well as in the Greek Old Testament,[26] so that the change of prepositions in verses 2b–3 seems to be merely stylistic. Thus Paul limits the "possession" of Christ's gift of grace first by referring to the eschatological glory of God which is still to be revealed in its fullness; the Christian's hope of receiving this glory is perfectly certain, and therefore he can boast in hope.[27] To this future glory Paul contrasts the present reality of Christian existence, which consists in *thlipsis.* Another glance at the concordance shows that Paul uses this word to mean "affliction" in a very broad sense, personal and universally human as well as specifically Christian affliction, so that the concept should probably be interpreted here in general terms (cf. Schlier). But this affliction that every Christian suffers is for Paul not a cause for complaining, but for boasting, because *thlipsis* gives rise to endurance, to character, and to hope that does not disappoint. The commentaries point out that Paul is here using the rhetorical form of the sorites (or "chain-syllogism") to express the paradox that it is *thlipsis,* which strengthens the Christian's hope for the coming glory. To understand this thought objectively one will first investigate the

Pauline sense of *kauchasthai*, making use primarily of the information in TDNT (III, 648ff.; R. Bultmann), and, second, one will bear in mind the proposition in verse 5*b*, which gives the reason for what has been said. For this proposition to be understood the meaning of the genitive in the construction *hē agapē tou theou* must be clear as well as the meaning of the "outpouring of the love of God into our hearts through the Holy Spirit."

The concordance shows that Paul uses the phrase *hē agapē tou theou* very infrequently (Romans 8:39, 2 Corinthians 13:13), but reference to Romans 5:8 and to the commentaries shows that in verse 5 Paul can only mean God's love toward us (and in the other two passages it is the same). The commentaries also indicate that the figure of the outpouring of the Holy Spirit is from the Old Testament, but that Paul varies it here so that the love of God is poured out, through the Spirit, into our hearts, by which he can only mean the certainty of God's love, which the Christian has received with the gift of the Spirit (cf. Michel). What Paul means by the "giving of the Holy Spirit" cannot, in fact, be learned from our passage, and it is plain that the expression can be made intelligible only if other Pauline expressions about the gift of the Spirit to Christians are compared with it. Here again a glance at the concordance is instructive (pointing, perhaps, to the parallels in 2 Corinthians 1:22; 5:5; 1 Thessalonians 4:8; Romans 8:11, 23; 1 Corinthians 3:16; 6:11), but in view of the fact that the doctrine of the Spirit permeates the whole of Pauline theology, it is advisable to refer at this point to a comprehensive discussion of Paul's views on the subject.[28] Then the connection of the gift of the Spirit with faith, baptism, and the actions of Christians will be clear.

Paul's interest in Romans 5:5, to be sure, is not in the gift of the Spirit but in the love of God, for in elucidating this concept he adds verses 6–8. Here again the first question to be thrashed out is the textual one, viz., whether *ei ge* at the beginning of verse 6 is to be regarded as the correct reading (so Nestle), since the majority of the "Egyptian" witnesses and good "Western" witnesses read *eti gar*. The apparatus shows that the manuscript tradition on this point is very complex, so the beginner must turn to the commentaries, all of which accept *eti gar* as the original reading. However, if one does accept this opinion, it remains uncertain how one should translate (cf. Schlier), and the only thing that is really clear is that Paul proves God's love for us with the statement that Christ died for the ungodly. And this meaning is confirmed by verse 8. In between, however, stands verse 7, the real *crux interpretum:* the first half of the sentence says that death on behalf of a righteous person hardly ever occurs (and, hence, it is implied that death on behalf of an unrighteous person *never* occurs), but the second half of the sentence states that death on behalf of a good person is entirely thinkable. Michel simply ignores this difficulty, and Käsemann and Schlier, in different ways, accept the second clause as a Pauline self-correction of the first. This verse cannot really be explained with any certainty, and we can only infer from it that Paul intends, in verse 8, to describe the divine love as something scarcely conceivable among human beings.

With verse 9, Paul brings together the main ideas of the two preceding sections: "We are justified by the death of Jesus," and once again he derives the hope for final salvation from the reality of this divine act. The expression *dikaiōthentes en tōi haimati autou* is not intelligible without further ado. With the help of the concordance one will, therefore, examine Paul's use of prepositions with *dikaiōthēnai* as well as his use of *haima,* and determine that Paul also connects *en* with *dikaioun* (Romans 3:4; 1 Corinthians 4:4; Galatians 3:11; 5:4), and by means of it indicates the facts that form the basis of justification. Furthermore, the parallel use of *haima* in Romans 3:25 and Colossians 1:20 shows that Paul uses *haima* as a sort of shorthand for "the death of Christ for our sins" (1 Corinthians 15:3).[29] For understanding verse 9, it is also important to be aware of Paul's frequent use of the argument *a minori ad maius* and to look up Michel's reference to Strack-Billerbeck.[30] A comparison of Paul's argumentation with the rabbinic prototype will show that in Paul there is no exegetical drawing out of conclusions but, rather, an argument arising out of the certainty of faith, which draws its consequences from the justification that is known in experience.

This experience of justification Paul now interprets in verses 10–11 by means of the concept of *reconciliation*. To understand the meaning of this idea we first compare (using the concordance) the linguistic usage of *katallassō* and *katallagē,* and thus we find that only 2 Corinthians 5:18–19 offers a true parallel; after this we examine the context of Romans 5:9–11. As a result of these inquiries, we see that for Paul the agent of reconciliation is God, just as he is also the agent of justification (which is therefore obviously the same thing). God effects the reconciliation of sinful, hostile mankind to himself through the death of Christ; the fact of reconciliation must be preached and accepted, and when accepted it imparts a real participation in the life of the risen Christ. If we wish to have a precise understanding of these ideas, we will first investigate the origin of the concept of reconciliation. The commentaries do not help us here, but the TDNT (I, 254; F. Büchsel) and Strack-Billerbeck (III, 519) show that the idea is met in early Judaism, but in the form of reconciling actions or prayers directed by men toward God. Moreover, the reference books and works on Pauline theology[31] tell us that Paul radically altered this idea, and that for Paul God himself effects reconciliation and makes it available, and that he does this, paradoxically, through the devotion of his Son in death (Romans 8:32). It is important that one should be clear that Paul, in this presentation, proclaims the reconciling action of God but makes no attempt to *explain* it.

Paul completes his train of thought in verse 11 by describing this reality that has been received in faith, this God-given reconciliation, as the foundation for the Christians' boasting that was referred to in verse 3 (Michel correctly calls attention to the repeated *nun* in verses 9 and 11): to boast of affliction and to boast of reconciliation by God are, therefore, obviously identical. A final exegetical problem is offered by the formula "[we boast] through our Lord Jesus Christ." Since the concluding relative clause of verse 11 (*di'hou,* etc.) describes Christ unequivocally as the agent and cause of God's reconciling act, it seems hard to refer the immediately preceding formula ("through our Lord Jesus Christ") to Christ as mediator of Christian boasting. Here a glance at Schlier's commentary[32] shows that clearly, here as in parallel statements of Paul, the sense is that we can boast with the help of the heavenly Lord God, because the Lord who died on the cross and rose again to heavenly life gives us, through his Spirit (5:5!), the possibility of boasting.

When we have tried to solve the exegetical problems of Romans 5:1–11 in the manner sketched here, the text should be accessible to us so that we can now not only translate it and understand the various concepts involved in it but also ask how it is addressed to us.

VII Exegesis of Matthew 12:22–37

As a second example, the exegesis of Matthew 12:22–37 will illustrate the procedure to be followed with a Synoptic text. For commentaries on this text, I choose Klostermann, Schweizer, and J. Schmid; and, in addition, the commentaries of Lohmeyer, Taylor, and Pesch on Mark, and those of Klostermann, Grundmann, and Rengstorf on Luke.[33]

The mention of the commentaries on Mark and Luke immediately shows that whenever a Synoptic text has parallels in one or both of the other Synoptics it is also necessary to consider these parallels. In the exegesis of a Synoptic text, it is therefore essential to take a Synopsis[34] as a point of departure and, in every case, to determine whether Synoptic parallels are present and whether they can contribute to the understanding of the text being interpreted.

There is no difficulty in determining the boundaries of the Matthean section. The preceding summary statement ends with 12:21, and the healing of the demoniac in 12:22 introduces the controversy about the power behind Jesus' works. It is also clear that a new section begins in 12:38, since the entrance of new parties to the discussion is indicated. The analysis of the section also confirms at least the first of these boundaries. First, after the amazement of the crowd at Jesus' healing of the deaf and dumb man, the Pharisees bring up the accusation that Jesus is in league with demons (verses 22–24). Jesus replies to this, making use of analogies (verses 25–26) to show the absurdity of this charge, pointing out the proper relationship of opponents to each other (verse 27) and explaining the true meaning of his power over demons (verse 28). Here the introduction of evidence seems to be over, but in spite of this a further analogy is introduced in verse 29 as another argument showing the absurdity of the charge that Jesus is in league with demons; verse 30 is probably intended to show the application of this. With this, however, the refutation of the accusation is finally finished; the saying about blasphemy against the Son of man and the Holy Spirit in verse 31 is, indeed, introduced by *dia touto,* but it is far from clear what this is supposed to refer back to. The sayings about the tree and the fruit (verses 33–35) and about the necessity for giving an account for idle words (verses 36–37) are even less obviously related to the foregoing discussion about being in league with demons, although no new beginning is recognizable before verse 38 (even if we prescind from the change in parties to the conversation in verse 38). Thus the analysis shows that the section is obviously put together out of several independent component parts, and that therefore it should not be taken for granted that the author of Matthew's Gospel expected the reader to understand it as a coherent unity. An exegesis that is meant to interpret the text in the evangelist's sense will, therefore, on the basis of the analysis of the text itself, be limited to making each separate component part of the text intelligible by itself.

If the text to be interpreted is not peculiar to Matthew, it is part of the exegetical task to take account of the parallels and to ask whether they can contribute anything to understanding the text; this is particularly true where Mark is to be supposed as a source for Matthew and Luke. Mark 3:22–30, which is parallel to Matthew 12:22–37, contains no account of a healing, but does begin with the charge about being in league with demons. Jesus shows the absurdity of this with the same analogies as in Matthew; however, the analogy of the Strong Man, which comes as a sort of afterthought or postscript in Matthew (12:29), follows without a break in Mark 3:27. Then follows in Mark 3:28–29 the statement that blasphemy against the Holy Spirit will not be forgiven, and here the addition of the saying is easily intelligible, since in verse 30 the blasphemy against the Holy Spirit is related to the charge of being in league with demons. With this the Marcan pericope ends; the sayings found in Matthew 12:23–37, whose connection with the charge of being in league with demons seemed so obscure, are, therefore, lacking in Mark. It goes without saying that if the Marcan text itself were being exegeted, one would have to ask whether it is not itself a composite section. In fact, this is quite probably true,[35] but this insight contributes nothing essential for understanding the Matthean text, since Matthew has obviously used this Marcan text, which, by itself, forms an intelligible coherent unity.

However, in the present case the Lucan parallels must

also be brought in, because a comparison of the wording shows that Luke is not dependent on Mark here, but has contacts with Matthew in those places where Matthew goes beyond Mark.[36] In Luke 11:14–23, the section dealing with the charge about being in league with demons appears not as a parallel to Mark 3:22ff. (Luke leaves this pericope out), but in his "travel narrative," in connection with a series of controversies with the Pharisees (cf. Rengstorf); this already suggests that Luke is following another tradition here. Luke 11:14ff. begins the pericope, as does Matthew, with a demon exorcism and the crowd's amazed (or abusive) reaction to it. The refutation of the charge by means of analogies and a correct interpretation of the healing of demoniacs follows in verses 17–20, but the wording of these verses corresponds not to Mark, but to Matthew: Luke puts the saying about the Strong Man (Matthew 12:29), which in Matthew has the effect of a sort of afterthought, into the same context as it has in Matthew, but with different wording (verses 21ff.), and, like Matthew, adds the not entirely appropriate application of verse 23. With this, the Lucan pericope ends. To be sure, Luke also has (in 12:10) a partial parallel to the Matthean (not the Marcan) form of the saying about blasphemy against the Son of man or against the Holy Spirit, and the sayings about the tree and the fruit occur in 6:43–45; however, both of these passages have quite different contexts.

The comparison of Matthew with Luke enables us to assert with confidence that Matthew 12:33–35 has in fact been taken over from another tradition and, with even more confidence, to draw this conclusion about verses 35ff., which are found only in Matthew. For Matthew 12:22–32, however, the comparison with Mark *and* Luke shows that Matthew has contacts alternately with Mark and Luke and, therefore, it is in the highest degree probable that the author of Matthew has combined the parallel versions, found in Mark and Q, of the pericope about the accusation of being in league with demons with the sayings there appended to it, and has added to this combination a further group of sayings from Q and one saying from his own special source. (The student should check this hypothesis, advanced on the basis of his own observations in the Synopsis, by reading the relevant portions of the commentaries of Schweizer, Schmid, and Pesch.)

From all of this a twofold conclusion follows for the exegesis of Matthew 12:22–37:

a) Whenever one cannot without difficulty recognize a chain of thought linking together the different component parts of a text, one must not assume that a connection exists; in such cases the primary purpose of the exegesis of a Synoptic Gospel, viz., the determination of the meaning that the evangelist has given to a text taken over by him, cannot be established with complete certainty.

b) The individual component parts of the section must, of course, first be interpreted as they stand in Matthew's version, but we must always bear in mind that a comparison with Mark and Luke may enable us to recognize a more original version of the tradition, and this will occasionally take us nearer to the meaning of the saying on the lips of Jesus.

It is in the light of these considerations that we may now attempt to arrive at an understanding of the Matthean text. The introductory scene (verses 22–24) offers no exegetical difficulties. The healing of the demoniac is interpreted by the crowd as a possible indication of Jesus' messiahship, but by the Pharisees it is ascribed to the assistance of Beelzebub, the prince of demons. Since Luke 11:14–15 contains essentially the same material, this form of the introduction to the controversy probably comes from the sayings-source Q, so that nothing of Matthew's editorial purpose can be learned from it.[37] Jesus' answer begins in verses 25–26 with the two analogies of the kingdom and of the city or house, which cannot stand if they are divided internally; from these it is deduced that a division in Satan's kingdom would have a similar result. Comparison with Mark and Luke shows that Matthew is here following Q, in general, but that he has added the example of the house from Mark, without thereby introducing any material change. In order to understand the sense of this argument against the possibility of Satan's kingdom being divided, one must know what ideas about demons and Satan were current in the New Testament period. This information can best be obtained by reading the articles *daimōn* and *satanas* in TDNT,[38] where it is shown that Jesus, in contrast to Jewish tradition, sees the demon world as completely subject to Satan; thus he, in contrast to his opponents, regards an internecine struggle within Satan's kingdom as unthinkable. Jesus knows only the *one* question, namely, whether God *or* Satan is at work in the event, and we must be aware of this rigidly monistic view of the Satanic realm in order to understand the connection with the following verses in Matthew.

Two sayings follow, in Matthew 12:27–28, which Matthew has in common only with Luke, but the connection with what precedes is immediately obvious only for verse 27. The point of verse 27 is clear when one learns from Klostermann that Jesus takes for granted the existence of Jewish exorcists and that "your sons" means, in fact, "your people." Thus Jesus is arguing that the Pharisees' accusation is disproved because they raise it only against him and not also against the exorcists in their own numbers. Beside this, however, in verse 28, Matthew places a saying whose meaning raises difficulties. A glance at the concordance shows that the verb *phthanein* occurs in the Synoptics only in this saying, and, hence, also never occurs elsewhere in connection with *basileia tou theou*. Its meaning can therefore be learned only from its use elsewhere in the New Testament or in profane writers, and in all other New Testament passages (with the exception of 1 Thessalonians 4:15, where it means "anticipate, come ahead of time") the meaning is clearly "arrive" (Bauer–Arndt–Gingrich's *Lexicon* and the commentaries con-

firm this).[39] The student will therefore have to find out
whether this saying can mean that the exorcisms that Jesus
performs by the power of God's Spirit are to be taken as an
actualization of God's kingdom among his hearers. A glance
at the otherwise verbally similar parallel in Luke 11:20 will
show him that Luke has "by the finger of God" instead of
"in the Spirit of God," but this is hardly a material difference (cf. Schweizer). Matthew therefore intends to say,
whether he has the original version here or not,[40] that Jesus
is acting in the power of the Spirit of God when he casts out
demons (and the concordance shows that Matthew has prepared for this understanding of Jesus' activity in 3:16; 4:1;
and 12:18). But if Jesus is maintaining, in verse 28, that his
casting out demons through the working of the Holy Spirit
proves that the kingdom of God has come, the connection of
12:28 to 12:27 can hardly be original, since the juxtaposition
of these two verses implies the doubtless unintentional result
that the Pharisaic demon exorcisms also prove the presence
of God's kingdom.[41]

Evidently, then, two sayings, which do not belong together, were already combined in the sayings-source used by
Matthew and Luke, and on this account one will not be able
to understand the Matthean text fully without investigating
the origin and original meaning of the individual sayings.
This form-critical inquiry, however, also leads one to ask
whether the sayings belong to the oldest traditions about Jesus and what meaning they had on Jesus' lips (in the event
that they do indeed come from him). The exegete of such a
Synoptic text must therefore take these form-critical and historical questions into consideration if he is to understand the
text in its process of development and in the sense finally
given to it by the evangelist. If the commentaries give no
bibliographical references to assist in following up such further questions, the beginner will have to look up the references given in lexica in the articles about Jesus, and he will

find, in the particular case we are dealing with, that the meaning of Matthew 12:28, as arrived at on the basis of New Testament linguistic usage, is regarded as doubtful by many scholars, because it does not square well with other sayings of Jesus about the *nearness* of God's kingdom, and that for this reason one should understand *ephthasen* to mean "has come near."[42] The exegete will have to test such a statement and, accordingly, decide whether or not he must alter his interpretation of the Matthean text.

When in Matthew 12:29 the saying about overpowering the Strong Man now follows as an argument against the charge of being in league with demons, it has the effect of an afterthought or postscript, as the analysis has already shown. A glance at the Marcan parallel shows that Matthew follows the Marcan text almost word for word, but since the same saying also occurs in this place in another versions in Luke 11:21–22, it obviously stood here in Q: from this it follows that the original context of Mark 3:26–27, which we have in Mark, has in Q been expanded by the addition of the material in Matthew 12:27–28 (which also appears in Luke 11:19–20). Since Matthew follows Q in the sequence of these verses, it is superfluous to look for a connection in thought between Matthew 12:28 and 12:29 as though deliberately intended by Matthew. Since no application of the saying about the Strong Man is given, one must be inferred; the commentaries on Matthew offer little help on this point, so that one must turn to commentaries on Mark 3:27 (cf. Taylor and Pesch). Again obviously following Q (cf. Luke 11:23), Matthew temporarily concludes this train of thought with the saying, "He who is not with me . . ." (12:30, which "warns against being uncommitted" (Klostermann). It is clear that this saying, which is in some way intended to refer to the necessity for following Jesus, does not originally belong in this context; what precise sense Matthew meant to give it is also unclear, since all indications are lacking. The commentaries discuss several possible explanations, but it is well to be aware that we have hardly anything here on which to base a certain interpretation.

The subject changes again, and there follows the double saying of Matthew 12:31–32, which first declares that all blasphemy is forgivable except that against the Spirit and then says that speaking against the Son of man is forgivable, but that speaking against the Holy Spirit is unforgivable. If we seek to understand this double saying in the context of Matthew's Gospel, we find that its connection with the preceding and following material is quite as obscure as the reason for the radically different valuation of rejecting the Son of man and rejecting the Holy Spirit; for it is not said that this double saying is supposed to be related to the charge of being in league with demons, and it can at most be *inferred* from the fact that the working of the Spirit in Jesus' demon exorcisms is mentioned in 12:28. Why speaking against the Son of man is described as forgivable in verse 32 can only be guessed at. Here too, of course, the exegete will take the Synoptic parallels into account before he turns to the commentaries, and he will notice first that Matthew combines the version of the saying in Mark 3:28–29 with that in Luke 12:10 (from Q); he will also notice, however, that Matthew has more strongly emphasized the *eternal* unforgivableness of speaking against the Holy Spirit. But, above all, he will notice that in Mark 3:28–29 the distinction between the Son of man and the Holy Spirit is lacking, and, furthermore, that Mark explicitly connects this saying with the accusation that Jesus is in league with demons. This comparison thus shows clearly that Matthew has been consciously composing here and, therefore, the contrast between the eternal unforgivableness of blasphemy against the Holy Spirit and the forgivability of blasphemy against the Son of man is obviously due to him. However, if one looks to the commentaries for help in understanding this contrast, one finds that every commentator offers a different explanation, since, in fact, we have no real possibility of answering this question.[43] The interpreter of Matthew must admit, for better or for worse, that the meaning of these two verses cannot be explained with any certainty, and then it only remains necessary to ask whether the version of the saying in Mark 3:28 is perhaps more original or, at least, more intelligible.[44] Thus, here again, the exegesis of Matthew leads necessarily to the problem of the oldest tradition and its relationship to Jesus.

In Matthew, there now follows (in 12:33–37) a loosely connected series of sayings whose relationship to what precedes is not immediately understandable. The discussion in Schmid's commentary shows that the saying about the tree and the fruit in verse 33 can apply equally well to Jesus (if the healings of demoniacs are not evil, then the one who performs them cannot be evil, and vice versa) and to the Pharisees (their calumny against Jesus proves that they are themselves evil; cf. verses 34–35). On the first interpretation, the *poiēsate* in verse 33 is easily understood, but the transition to verses 34–35 is awkward, since these verses *must* refer to the Pharisees; on the second interpretation the *poiēsate* is difficult, and one must understand it in a weakened sense ("suppose the tree is good . . ."[45]) which gives a unity to verses 33–35 in that they then all deal with the true nature of the Pharisees. Since it seems impossible to decide for one interpretation or the other in the context of Matthew, one will again turn to the Lucan parallel 6:43–45, which comes at the end of the Lucan Sermon on the Plain. In wording (but not altogether in the order of the words) it corresponds by and large to Matthew 12:33–35; the Matthean parallel to Luke 6:44b ("Figs are not gathered from thorns . . ."), however, is not found here, but at the end of the Sermon on the Mount (Matthew 7:16b), and Matthew 12:34a ("You brood of vipers! how can you speak good, when you are evil?") has no parallel in Luke. Now it is hardly possible to give a straightforward explanation of the relationship of the three texts (Matthew 12:33–35, its parallel in Luke 6:43–45, and Matthew 7:16–18, 20) to one another,[46] but the comparison just made leads us to suppose that the extra material in Matthew 12:34a was added to the tradition by Matthew (see Klostermann, and Bultmann, *History of the Synoptic Tradition,* p. 95[2]), and, hence, it is likely that Matthew applied verse 33 to the Pharisees. In this case, therefore, the Synoptic comparison helps us to reach a more certain interpretation of the Matthean text.

Matthew concludes the entire section in verses 36–37 with a saying about the enduring consequences of human speech; this has no Synoptic parallel and is, therefore, from Matthew's special source. Though the saying is quite general in its formulation, Matthew has probably applied it to the Pharisees for having accused Jesus of being in league with demons, and in this connection Klostermann's commentary refers to A. Jülicher,[47] who, among others, interprets *rhēma argon* as "invective," on the basis of a supposed Aramaic original. Here, however, one must proceed with proper attention to exegetical method. Since Matthew elsewhere uses *argos* only once, and then with the meaning "idle" (20:3), we have no reason to ascribe the sense "abusive" to the evangelist, especially since he probably took over this saying in the Greek language. At most, then, one could understand the meaning suggested by Klostermann as an older sense of the saying found *before* Matthew. But since the saying is formulated in quite general terms, one will have to suppose a more general meaning for even the pre-Matthean sense of the saying, and the student can discover from Strack-Billerbeck (I, 693) that similar sayings were made by the rabbis, and, from TDNT (I, 452, s.v. *argos*), that *argos* in Matthew 12:36 is, in the context of verse 34, to be interpreted as synonymous with *ponēros* = worthless."[48] Whether or not this meaning is appropriate in the context of Jesus' discourse, or whether one should perhaps refuse to attribute this saying to Jesus, or whether one should give it, hypothetically, another meaning on Jesus' lips, are questions that exegesis cannot answer, but that the exegete must not evade, if he wishes to understand the saying of Jesus in its existential meaning. Here again exegesis leads of necessity to biblical theology and, therefore, also to the historical question about the outlook of Jesus, of Paul, etc. But to embark upon these methodological researches is not the task of this introductory methodological guide for beginners.

NOTES FOR OLD TESTAMENT
EXEGESIS

1. Full bibliographical data will be repeated when the writer judges this advantageous to the reader. The bibliography is far more extensive in this edition than in previous ones, due chiefly to a desire to introduce the student to the relevant work done in recent years in language, literary theory, and scientific theory.

2. G. Fohrer in his *Theologische Grundstrukturen des Alten Testaments* (Berlin and New York, 1972), pp. 95ff., sees in this the factor that brings unity into the multiplicity of Old Testament statements. It seems to me that the same can be said of the New Testament and the testimonies of Church history. In my view, it is also helpful for a theological understanding of Judaism and Islam.

3. Cf. E. Brunner, *Reason and Revelation* (Philadelphia, 1946), pp. 118ff.; K. Barth, *Evangelical Theology: An Introduction,* tr. by G. Foley (New York, 1963), pp. 15–25; H. Grass, *Christliche Glaubenslehre* II (ThW 12, 2; Stuttgart, 1974), pp. 72ff.

4. On this, cf. G. Ratschow, *Der angefochtene Glaube* (Gütersloh, 1957; 1960[2]), pp. 216ff., and H. Diem, *Dogmatics,* tr. by H. Knight (Philadelphia, 1959).

5. For information, cf. E. G. Kraeling, *The Old Testament since the Reformation* (London, 1955); H.-J. Kraus, *Geschichte der historisch-Kritischen Erforschung des Alten Testaments* (Neukirchen, 1969[2]); W. G. Kümmel, *The New Testament: The History of the Investigation of Its Problems,* tr. by S. M. Gilmour and H. C. Kee (Nashville, 1972). For the theological significance of the critical historical method and for the problems it raises, cf. G. Ebeling, "The Significance of the Critical Historical Method for Church and Theology in Protestantism," in his *Word and Faith,* tr.

by J. W. Leitch (Philadelphia, 1963), pp. 17–61; W. Pannenberg, *Theology and the Philosophy of Science,* tr. by F. McDonagh (Philadelphia, 1976), pp. 381–90. On the Catholic side, cf., e.g., K. Lehmann, in J. Schreiner (ed.), *Einführung in die Methoden der biblischen Exegese* (Würzburg, 1971), pp. 62ff., and J. Gnilka, "Methodik und Hermeneutik," in *Neues Testament und Kirche: Festschrift für R. Schnackenburg* (Freiburg, Basel, and Vienna, 1974), pp. 458ff.

6. Cf. also E. D. Hirsch, Jr., *Prinzipien der Interpretation* (UTB 104; Munich, 1972), pp. 263ff. [This is a translation of *Validity in Interpretation* [New Haven, 1967], which was unavailable to me; page references will therefore be to the German version. —Tr.]

7. On this subject, cf. also R. Bultmann, "Is Exegesis without Presuppositions Possible?" in his *Existence and Faith: Shorter Writings of Rudolf Bultmann,* tr. by S. M. Ogden (New York, 1960), pp. 289–96.

8. O. F. Bollnow, "Was heisst, einen Schriftsteller besser zu verstehen, als er sich selber verstanden hat?" in *Das Verstehen: Drei Aufsätze zur Theorie des Geisteswissenschaften* (Mainz, 1949), p. 25. Cf. also Pannenberg, op. cit., ch. 3.

9. On this subject, cf. the facts and reflections in H. Grass, *Christliche Glaubenslehre* II, pp. 92ff, or G. Ebeling, *The Study of Theology,* tr. by D. A. Priebe (Philadelphia, 1978), ch. 3. For Old Testament hermeneutics, cf. H. Seebass, *Biblische Hermeneutik* (Urban TB 199; Stuttgart, 1974), and A. H. J. Gunneweg, *Understanding the Old Testament,* tr. by J. Bowden (Philadelphia, 1978).

10. On this subject, cf. R. Ingarden, *The Literary Work of Art* (Evanston, 1973), as well as E. Leibfried, *Kritische Wissenschaft vom Text* (Stuttgart, 1970), p. 85. That a multiplicity of meanings in a text does not invalidate the distinction between a correct and an erroneous interpretation is explained in Hirsch, op. cit., p. 264, who uses the example of the musical rendition of a score. On this point, cf. also Leibfried, op. cit., p. 87. On the philosophical background in the phenomenology of E. Husserl for the approaches of Ingarden, Hirsch, and Leibfried, cf. G. Pasternack, *Theoriebildung in der Literaturwissenschaft* (UTB 426; Munich, 1975), pp. 56ff., and W. Stegmüller, *Hauptströmungen der Gegenwartsphilosophie* 1 (Stuttgart, 1975⁴), pp. 81ff.

11. On this point, cf. Bultmann, op. cit., pp. 293–95. On Bultmann's approach to hermeneutics, cf. W. Schmithals, *An Introduction to the Theology of Rudolf Bultmann*, tr. by J. Bowden (Minneapolis, 1968[2]), ch. 11. For information on the existential ontology of Heidegger cf., e.g., W. Weischedel, *Die philosophische Hintertreppe* (Munich, 1973[3]), pp. 329ff., or Stegmüller, op. cit., pp. 135ff. and 177ff. For criticism of Bultmann's concept of preunderstanding, cf. also Leibfried, op. cit., pp. 49ff.

12. Since, to use the language of textual linguistics, the fictional or nonfictional character of a text can find expression at least in its linguistic form (cf., e.g., E. Werlich, *Typologie der Texte* [UTB 450; Heidelberg, 1975], pp. 19ff. and 99ff.), it is not possible to avoid the problem of historicity by falling back on an ''interpretation of the work'' approach. But, entirely apart from this consideration, an appropriate understanding of a text is possible only when the question of its real horizon is answered; an evasion of this question is therefore an improper abridgment of the exegetical task. To say this is, however, to make no decision on who can or should be more competent than the exegete to answer the question. To call a narrative a ''faith-inspired tale'' (*Glaubensfabulat*) or an ''etiological tale'' (*Aitionfabulat*)—two terms, not otherwise common in Old Testament scholarship, which C. W. von Sydow uses in his ''Kategorien der Prosa-Volksdichtung'' (1934) in L. Petzold (ed.), *Vergleichende Sagenforschung* (WdF 152; Darmstadt, 1969), pp. 79ff., and which I repeat for explanation of the problem—or a saga or an annalistic account is at the same time to evaluate the horizon of reality and to exclude an inappropriate historical interpretation on the part of the modern reader. The language of the critical historical method, contrary to what W. Richter says in his *Exegese als Literaturwissenschaft. Entwurf einer alttestamentlichen Literaturtheorie und Methodologie* (Göttingen, 1971), pp. 17ff., is not conditioned by the approach it took in the beginning and has therefore not been rendered meaningless today. Richter, who is concerned with the establishment of the first stages of exegesis, has provoked not unjustified critical questions regarding his own position on the historical task of the exegete, from H. Barth and O. H. Steck, *Exegese des Alten Testaments. Leitfaden der Methodik* (Neukirchen, 1978[8]), pp. 74ff.; cf. also K. Koch in *ThLZ* 98 (1973), cols. 809 and 812. The ''interpretation of the work'' approach has

also found in W. Richter its strongest supporter in German Old Testament scholarship, after it had been especially introduced by L. Alonso-Schökel, cf. VTS 7 (Leiden, 1960), pp. 154ff., and in his *The Inspired Word: Scripture in the Light of Language and Literature* tr. by F. Martin (New York, 1963) [translated into German as *Sprache Gottes und der Menschen* (Düsseldorf, 1968)], and acquired an influence due to the translation of Alonso-Schökel's *Estudios de poética hebrea* (1963) as *Das Alte Testament als literarisches Kunstwerk* (Cologne, 1971) and due also to Richter's methodology. The same approach has been independently adopted by M. Weiss as a supplement to traditional methods; cf. VTS 22 (Leiden, 1972), p. 90, n. 1, and p. 89, n. 3. For the history of the "interpretation of the work" approach, cf. Leibfried, op. cit., pp. 188ff.

13. On this subject, cf. G. Ebeling, "Church History as the History of the Exposition of Scripture," in his *The Word of God and Tradition: Historical Studies Interpreting the Divisions of Christianity,* tr. by S. H. Hooke (Philadelphia, 1968), pp. 11–31.

14. On this subject, cf., e.g., A. Weiser, "Vom Verstehen des Alten Testaments," ZAW 61 (1945–48), 17ff., also contained in his *Glaube und Geschichte im Alten Testament* (Göttingen, 1961), pp. 290ff. Contrary to H. Gese, "Erwägungen zur Einheit der biblischen Theologie," AThK 67 (1970), 423, also contained in his *Vom Sinai zum Zion* (Munich, 1974), p. 17, I am not convinced that demonstrating the unity of the biblical tradition resolves "the dubious question of the Christian interpretation of the Old Testament." My reason for saying this is that this process is marked by inherent tensions (as a consideration of Judaism shows) and polyvalences and is itself subject to historical changes of meaning.

15. In my view, the postulate of a unitary biblical theology—on this, cf. Pannenberg, op. cit., pp. 381–90—can only be verified at the present time by an improved collaboration between Old Testament and New Testament exegetes. Contrary to the view of Pannenberg, op. cit., pp. 389–90, and others, for objective reasons Old Testament scholars cannot but continue in isolation to carry on their work in literary, secular, and religious history. The reason is that the findings needed for a synthesis are not yet available. A

synthetic comprehensive picture that corresponds in an appropriate way to the course of history as we know it is indeed the ultimate goal of the separate areas of research, but the goal may not be elevated to the position of an obligatory model for teaching and other forms of presentation, since a critical stance with regard to it is possible only as long as the more limited problems of basic research are familiar to every theologian.

16. On this point, cf. C. H. Ratschow, *Die Bedeutung der Theologie für Kirche und Gemeinde* (Glauben and Leben 3; Bad Salzuflen, 1963), pp. 46ff.

17. The handy edition of the Hebrew Bible that N. H. Snaith edited for the British and Foreign Bible Society is based on a manuscript of the year 1485 and takes into account two other mss. from the fourteenth and fifteenth centuries. These witnesses are primarily in the same tradition as the Codex Leningradensis.

18. Tübingen, I, 1922; II, 1923[4] (reprint ed., Darmstadt, 1971).

19. Help in its use can be gotten from K. Huber and H. H. Schmid, *Zürcher Bibel Konkordanz* I–III (Olten, 1969–74).

20. Tübingen, 1900, 1921; reprint ed., Darmstadt, 1962.

21. Oxford, 1913, 1968.

22. Augsburg, 1928; reprint ed., Heidelberg, 1966[2], and Gütersloh, 1973ff.

23. Darmstadt, 1971[2]. The best English translation of the Qumran texts is probably G. Vermes, *The Dead Sea Scrolls in English* (Baltimore, 1962).

24. Still to be considered basic is the *Hebräisches und Aramäisches Handwörterbuch über das Alte Testament* of W. Gesenius. Corresponding to it in English is F. Brown, S. R. Driver, and C. A. Briggs (eds.), *A Hebrew and English Lexicon of the Old Testament; with an Appendix Containing the Biblical Aramaic;* based on the lexicon of Gesenius as translated by E. Robinson (Oxford, 1953). The progress since made in lexicography can be seen in L. Köhler and W. Baumgartner, *Lexicon in Veteris Testamenti Libros* (Leiden, 1958[2]). The revision of this by W. Baumgartner as *Hebräisches und Aramäisches Lexikon zum Alten Testament* has reached *nbṭ* in the two fascicles thus far published: 1 (Leiden, 1967) and 2 (Leiden, 1974); in the future this will be an indis-

pensable work. Again, there is a related work in English: *Concise Hebrew and Aramaic Lexicon of the Old Testament, Based Upon the Lexical Work of Ludwig Koehler and Walter Baumgartner*, by W. L. Holladay (Grand Rapids, 1971). There is a pocket dictionary, G. Fohrer (ed.) *Hebrew and Aramaic Dictionary of the Old Testament*, tr. by W. Johnstone (Berlin, 1973), but since this does not list the forms attested or give references to scripture, it cannot simply be substituted for the works listed above, but at best can only replace them in certain situations.

25. B. Davidson's *Analytical Hebrew and Chaldee Lexicon* (London, 1974) is meant for students who have difficulty in determining the noun and verb forms in Hebrew and Aramaic. In addition to using his textbook on grammar, the student should also consult, for its extensive indexes if nothing else, W. Gesenius and E. Kautzsch, *Hebräische Grammatik* (Leipzig, 1909[28]) and the first two parts of the 29th edition edited by G. Bergsträsser (Leipzig 1918–29; reprint ed., Hildesheim, 1962). This work is easily accessible in the English-language edition edited by A. Cowley (Oxford, 1910, 1960). The student can derive supplementary help from P. Joüon, *Grammaire de l'Hebreu biblique* (Rome, 1923, 1965) and, above all, the *Hebräische Grammatik* I–IV, of R. Meyer (Berlin, 1966–72[3]). On Hebrew syntax, always a thorny subject, there is C. Brockelmann, *Hebräische Syntax* (Neukirchen, 1956); the *Hebrew Syntax* of B. Davidson (Edinburgh, 1901[3], 1971) still has its value. A new outline of the syntax of the verb is given in the doctoral dissertation of H. Bobzin, *Die "Tempora" im Hiobdialog* (Marburg, [1974] 1975), based on the approach developed by O. Rössler of Marburg.

For the Aramaic sections of the Old Testament, I may mention F. Rosenthal, *A Grammar of Biblical Aramaic* (Wiesbaden, 1961, 1963), in addition to the older works of H. Bauer and P. Leander: *Grammatik des Biblisch-Aramäischen* (Halle, 1927; reprint ed., Hildesheim, 1962) and *Kurzgefasste Biblisch-Aramäische Grammatik* (Halle, 1929).

A survey of the system of Semitic languages can be gotten with the help of G. Bergsträsser, *Einführung in die semitischen Sprachen* (Munich, 1928; reprint ed., Darmstadt, 1963, with an appendix by G. Brockelmann, "Zur Syntax der Sprache von

Ugarit''), or of S. Moscati (ed.), *An Introduction to the Comparative Grammar of the Semitic Languages* (Wiesbaden, 1969). For a deeper understanding of Hebrew morphology, H. Bauer and P. Leander, *Historische Grammatik der Hebräischen Sprache des Alten Testaments* (Halle, 1922; reprint ed., Hildesheim, 1962), is still indispensable. On the Aramaisms of the Bible, cf. M. Wagner, *Die lexikalischen und grammatikalischen Aramaismen im alttestamentlichen Hebräisch* (BZAW 96; Berlin, 1966).

26. A. Rahlfs, *Septuaginta,* 2 vols. (Stuttgart, 1935; 1965[8]); B. Fischer et al., *Biblia Sacra iuxta vulgatam versionem,* 2 vols. (Stuttgart, 1969). Indispensable for truly scientific textual criticism are A. E. Brooke, N. McLean, and H. J. Thackeray, *The Old Testament in Greek* (Cambridge, 1906–40), and the edition sponsored by the Societas Litterarum Gottingensis, *Septuaginta. Vetus Testamentum Graecum* (Göttingen, 1926ff.). Both editions are still incomplete, and no continuation of the Cambridge edition can be anticipated, at least at the present time. The Cambridge Septuagint prints a single unaltered ms. and puts the rest of the material into the apparatus for the reader's own judgment. Rahlfs and the Göttingen edition, which derives its principles from him, print a revised critical text, while again putting the evidence in the apparatus for the readers to form their own judgment.

27. A. v. Gall, *Der hebräische Pentateuch der Samaritaner* (Giessen, 1914–28; reprint ed., Berlin, 1963). On this work, cf. O. Kaiser, *Introduction to the Old Testament,* tr. by J. Sturdy (Minneapolis, 1977[3]).

28. For an introduction, cf. F. M. Cross, *The Ancient Library of Qumran* (London, 1958), and the bibliography in Chr. Burchard, *Bibliographie zu den Handschriften vom Toten Meer* 1 (BZAW 76; Berlin, 1957, 1959[2]) and 2 (BZAW 89; Berlin, 1965). A classification of the mss. and editions of the nonbiblical material from Qumran is given by K. Müller in J. Schreiner (ed.), *Einführung in die Methoden der biblischen Exegese* (Würzburg, 1971), pp. 303ff. A list of the biblical Hebrew texts found at Qumran is given in G. Fohrer, *Introduction to the Old Testament* (Nashville, 1968[10]). An outline of the literary history is available henceforth in H. Lichtenberger, *Studien zum Menschenbild in den Texten der Qumrangemeinde* (Marburg dissertation, 1975).

29. *Biblia Sacra Polyglotta* I–VI (London, 1657; reprint ed., Graz, 1964).

30. Cf., e.g., O. Eissfeldt, *The Old Testament: An Introduction,* tr. by P. R. Ackroyd (New York, 1965), pp. 669ff.; A. Weiser, *The Old Testament: Its Formation and Development,* tr. by D. M. Barton (New York, 1961), pp. 351–68; Fohrer, Introduction or R. Smend, *Die Entstehung des Alten Testaments* (ThWi 1; Stuttgart, 1978), pp. 20ff.

31. Cf. P. Kahle, *The Cairo Geniza* (Oxford, 1959[2]); idem, *Die Kairoer Geniza* (Berlin, 1962); F. M. Cross, "The Contribution of the Qumran Discoveries to the Study of the Biblical Text," *Israel Exploration Journal* 16 (1966): 81ff.; H. B. Swete, R. R. Ottley, and H. St. Thackeray, *An Introduction to the Old Testament in Greek* (Cambridge, 1914; 1968); S. Jellicoe, *The Septuagint and Modern Study* (Oxford, 1968); J. Ziegler, *Sylloge. Gesammelte Aufsätze zur Septuaginta* (Göttingen, 1971); B. Kedar-Kopfstein, *The Vulgate as a Translation* (Jerusalem dissertation, 1968); F. Stummer, *Einführung in die lateinischen Bibel* (Paderborn, 1928).

32. Oxford, 1957; 3rd German ed., Berlin, 1962, 1974.

33. *The Text of the Old Testament: An Introduction to the Biblia Hebraica,* 2nd English ed., tr. by E. F. Rhodes from the 4th German ed. of 1973 (Grand Rapids, 1979).

34. Cf. ibid., pp. 11ff.

35. Cf. notes 31 and 33.

36. This indispensable tool for scholarly work on the Old Testament is available in a reprint (Graz, 1955) and in an edition by M. H. Goshen-Gottstein (Jerusalem, 1971[9]). G. Lisowsky's *Konkordanz zum Hebräischen Alten Testament* (Stuttgart, 1966[2]) has special but on the whole limited value.

37. For the pertinent lexicons, cf. below, p. 104, n. 4.

38. Reprint ed., Graz, 1954.

39. If difficulties arise in determining the forms of the Greek verbs, help can be obtained from G. Traut, *Lexikon über die Formen der griechischen Verba* (Giessen, 1867; reprint ed., Darmstadt, 1973[4]).

40. Cf. the reflections of A. Jepson, "Von den Aufgaben der Textkritik," in *Congress Volume, Bonn 1962* (Leiden, 1963), pp.

332ff., and of M. H. Goshen-Gottstein, *The Book of Isaiah: Sample Edition with Introduction* (Jerusalem, 1965), pp. 11ff., and Würthwein, pp. 103–4.

41. Cf. the explanation of "text" given by E. Werlich, *Typologie der Texte* (Heidelberg, 1975): "By 'textual utterances' ('texts' for short) we understand . . . those linguistic utterances that are characterized by (superimposed strata of) *coherence* and *completeness* in the sequence of their linguistic unities" (p. 17).

42. On this point, cf. also Würthwein, op. cit., pp. 21–22, and, for an example, K. Elliger, *Jesaja II* (Neukirchen, 1978), pp. 242ff.

43. For this, cf. the works mentioned in notes 26, 27, and 30. In addition, cf. K. Koch, *The Form-Critical Method,* tr. by S. M. Cupitt from the 2nd German ed. (New York, 1969) [there is now a third German ed., Neukirchen, 1974]; J. Schreiner, "Formen und Gattungen im Alten Testament," in J. Schreiner (ed.), *Einführung in die Methoden der biblischen Exegese* (Würzburg, 1971), pp. 194ff. Especially suitable for a first encounter with the problem is F. Stolz, *Interpreting the Old Testament,* tr. by M. Kohl (London, 1975), where the beginner will also find a clear guide to the history of the research and to the concrete problems of literary criticism.

44. On this, cf. M. Weiss, "Die Methode der 'Total-Interpretation,' " in *Congress Volume, Uppsala 1972* (VTS 22; Leiden, 1972), pp. 88ff. We could dismiss the problem of linguistic structuralism with a quotation from R. Barthes in X. Léon-Dufour (ed.), *Exegese im Methodenkonflikt* (Munich, 1973) [tr. of *Exégèse et herméneutique* (Paris, 1971)], p. 141, where he tells us that "the purpose of this type of investigation is not to explain or interpret the text but to query the text [the example used is Acts 10–11] with a view to establishing a universal language of narrative." Such a dismissal, however, would simply be the easy way out. There is an informative report on the subject that stirs the curiosity of the exegete, and I refer the reader to it: T. Todorov, "Poetik," in F. Wahl (ed.), *Einführung in den Strukturalismus* (Frankfurt am Main, 1973), pp. 105ff. [tr. of *Qu'est-ce que le structuralisme?* (Paris, 1968)], and in H. Naumann (ed.), *Der moderne Strukturbegriff. Materialien zu seiner Entwicklung* (WdF 155; Darmstadt, 1973).

For an example of the acceptance and application of this approach, cf. R. Lack, "Le sacrifice d'Isaac. Analyse structurale de la couche elohiste dans Gn 22," Bibl 56 (1975): 1ff.

45. On this, cf. H. Bobzin, *Die "Tempora" im Hiobdialog* (1974 dissertation; Marburg, 1975), p. 34; A. Denz, *Die verbalsyntax des neuarabischen Dialektes von Kwayris (Irak). Mit einer allgemeinen Tempus- und Aspektlehre* (AKM 40, 1; Wiesbaden, 1971), pp. 39ff.; K. Bühler, *Sprachtheorie* (Stuttgart, 1965²), pp. 28–29.

46. Cf. Richter, *Exegese als Literaturwissenschaft* (Göttingen, 1971), pp. 79ff., and G. Wanke, in G. Fohrer (ed.), *Exegese des Alten Testaments* (UTB 267; Heidelberg, 1976²), pp. 57ff., with the example given on pp. 176ff. and the table following p. 182. I must explicitly emphasize the point that Richter and Wanke would have this form criticism or linguistic analysis come after literary criticism, because they are primarily interested in the linguistic aspect. For a discussion of the approach, cf., in addition to the reservations voiced by H. Barth, O. H. Steck, and K. Koch (n. 12, above), the endorsements of W. Schenk, "Die Aufgaben der Exegese und die Mittel der Linguistik," ThLZ 98 (1973): 881ff., and J. Gnilka, in *Festschrift für Rudolf Schnackenburg* (1974), p. 470. On the subject, cf. W. Dressler, *Einführung in die Textlinguistik* (Konzepte der Sprach- und Literaturwissenschaft 13; Tübingen, 1973²); for a discussion of the textual linguistic method, cf. S. J. Schmidt, *Textlinguistik* (UTB 202; Munich, 1973), as well as the approach of E. Werlich, *Typologie der Texte* (UTB 450; Heidelberg, 1975).

47. As examples, cf. W. Richter, *Traditionsgeschichtliche Untersuchungen zum Richterbuch* (BBB 18; Bonn, 1963); H. Schulz, *Das Buch Nahum* (BZAW 129; Berlin and New York, 1973); and J. Garscha, *Studien zum Ezechielbuch* (EHS.T 23; Bern and Frankfurt am Main, 1974).

48. Cf. the works listed in notes 26, 27, and 30.

49. On this point, cf. W. Porzig, *Das Wunder der Sprache. Problem, Methoden und Ergebnisse der Sprachwissenschaft* (UTB 32; Munich, 1971⁵), p. 121. On the problem of the concept of literary style, cf. also W. Kayser, *Das sprachliche Kunstwerk* (Bern and Munich, 1959⁵), pp. 71ff. On mathematical methods in

literary scholarship, cf. E. Leibfried, *Kritische Wissenschaft vom Text* (Stuttgart, 1970), pp. 178–79.

50. Cf. n. 12, above. For what follows, cf. especially E. König, *Stilistik, Rhetorik, Poetik in bezug auf die biblische Litteratur* (Leipzig, 1900); Kayser, op. cit., pp. 100ff.; L. Alonso-Schökel, *Das Alte Testament als literarisches Kunstwerk* (Cologne, 1971) [tr. of *Estudios de poética hebrea* (Barcelona, 1963)]; for a general introduction, cf. Kaiser, *Introduction*.

51. Cf. G. Hölscher, *Geschichtsschreibung in Israel. Untersuchungen zum Jahvisten und Elohisten* (Lund, 1952), pp. 209ff. On the importance of the study of stylistics for literary criticism, cf. now F. Deist, "Stilvergleichung als literarkritisches Verfahren," ZAW 89 (1977):325ff.

52. I may mention here alliteration (repetition of individual letters or groups of letters with the same sound), alphabetical acrostics, paronomasia (occurrence of words with the same sound), onomatopoeia (painting pictures with sounds), and rhyme (homoioteleuton).

53. For example, parallelismus membrorum, merism (description by polarities), enumeration, repetition, and ellipsis.

54. These include, e.g., synonymy, antithesis, litotes (expression of something positive by denial of its opposite), irony (what is intended is the opposite of what is said), metonymy (designating one thing by means of another to which it is related by some internal quality), synecdoche (designating one thing by means of another to which it is related by some external quality), euphemism, allusion, hyperbole (exaggeration), image, comparison, and finally metaphor (transferral of meaning from one sphere to another). Evidently, the correctness of our approach to an allusion or a metaphor is limited by the fact that our knowledge of Hebrew is solely derived from lexicons and concordances. A distinction between genuinely metaphorical language and a secondary transferral of meaning that has become part of everyday speech can often be made only after careful semantic study. On this point, cf. also S. Ullmann, *The Principles of Semantics* (Oxford, 1957).

55. But cf. also Richter, *Exegese*, pp. 99ff.

56. Cf. below, p. 20ff.

57. Cf. Th. Willi, *Die Chronik als Auslegung* (FRLANT 106;

Göttingen, 1972), p. 172. There is a good example of the mosaic style in Judges 13:2ff.

58. E. Harder and R. Paret, *Kleine Arabische Sprachlehre* (Heidelberg, 1969), p. 16, §11, 1.

59. Cf. the review of the history of research and the discussion in Alonso-Schökel, op. cit. (n. 50), pp. 77–190. For an understanding of the terminology that has been taken over from classical metrics, the theologian will find valuable help in K. Rupprecht, *Einführung in die griechische Metrik* (Munich, 1950[3]).

60. Cf. Richter, *Exegese*, pp. 72ff.; but also F. Sengle, *Die literarische Formenlehre* (Stuttgart, 1969[2]), and, for discussion in terms of the literary disciplines, K. W. Hempfer, *Gattungstheorie* (UTB 133; Munich, 1973).

61. See the program given by H. Gunkel, *Die Israelitische Literatur* (Kultur der Gegenwart 1, 7; Leipzig, 1925; reprint ed., Darmstadt, 1963) and the literary–historical discussion in J. Hempel, *Die althebräische Literatur und ihr hellenistisch-jüdisches Nachleben* (Wildberg and Potsdam, 1930–34; reprint ed., Berlin, 1968[2]) and A. Lods, *Histoire de la littérature hébraïque et juive depuis les origines à la ruine de l'état juive (135 après J.-C.)* (Paris, 1950). It is worth noting that T. Todorov, "Poetik" (no. 44, above), pp. 164ff., in discussing a structural science of literature, works out an analogous program for the history of literature as a history of the evolution of the special characteristics both of literary language (i.e., in fact, of the genres!) and, as a preliminary, of its components. For an introduction to the problems of genre study, cf. the introductions mentioned in notes 26, 27, and 30 and the further literature mentioned in n. 43.

62. Cf. above, p. 21.

63. Cf. O. Kaiser, *Isaiah 13–39* (Philadelphia: Old Testament Library, 1974). There is a second German edition (ATD 18; Göttingen, 1976), pp. 173–79 and the commentary on the passages indicated.

64. W. Kayser, *Das sprachliche Kunstwerk* (Bern and Munich, 1959[5]), p. 60; cf. pp. 59ff. By "trait" (*Zug*) is meant "the concrete individual details of a motif" (p. 60). Thus, for example, in the confidence motif of a psalm of lament or supplication are found as traits the expressions of trust, hope, and fearlessness; cf. Ps 56:4–5.

65. Cf. ibid., p. 77.

66. Cf. ibid., p. 79.

67. Cf. above, pp. 3–4. For discussion, cf. Richter, *Exegese,* pp. 125ff., and Kaiser, *Introduction.*

68. Cf. also T. Veijola, *Das ewige Dynastie. David und die Entstehung seiner Dynastie nach der deuteronomistischen Darstellung* (AASF, Ser. B 193; Helsinki, 1975).

69. Cf. also H.-J. Hermisson, *Studien zur israelitischen Spruchweisheit* (WMANT 28; Neukirchen, 1968), pp. 133ff.; and on the problem, cf. R. N. Whybray, *The Intellectual Tradition in the Old Testament* (BZAW 135; Berlin and New York, 1974).

70. To familiarize themselves with the *history of Israel,* students may turn to the presentations by R. Kittel, *Geschichte des Volkes Israel* 1 (Stuttgart, 1932[7]), 2 (1925[7]), 3 (1927–29); M. Noth, *The History of Israel,* tr. by S. Godman (New York, 1960[2]); J. Bright, *A History of Israel* (Philadelphia, 1972[2]); R. de Vaux, *The Early History of Israel,* tr. by D. Smith (Philadelphia, 1978) (down to the period of the Judges); A. H. J. Gunneweg, *Geschichte Israels bis Bar Kochba* (ThW 2; Stuttgart, 1979[3]); M. Metzger, *Grundriss der Geschichte Israels* (Neukirchen, 1977[4]); S. Hermann, *A History of Israel in Old Testament Times,* tr. by J. Bowden (Philadelphia, 1975); F.-M. Abel, *Histoire de la Palestine depuis la conquête d'Alexandre jusqu'à l'invasion arabe,* 2 vols. (Paris, 1952).

On *Israelite–Jewish theology and religious history,* cf. W. Eichrodt, *Theology of the Old Testament,* tr. by J. A. Baker, 1 (London, 1961), 2 (1967); L. Köhler, *Old Testament Theology,* tr. by A. S. Todd (Philadelphia, 1957); G. von Rad, *Old Testament Theology,* tr. by D. M. G. Stalker, 1 (New York, 1962), 2 (1965); W. Zimmerli, *Old Testament Theology in Outline,* tr. by D. Green (Atlanta, 1978[2]); Fohrer, *Theologische Grundstrukturen des Alten Testaments* (Berlin, 1972); idem, *History of Israelite Religion,* tr. by D. E. Green (Nashville, 1973. [There is a 2nd German ed., 1973.]); H. Ringgren, *Israelite Religion,* tr. by D. E. Green (Philadelphia, 1966); W. H. Schmidt, *Alttestamentlicher Glaube in seiner Geschichte* (Neukirchen, 1975[2]); C. Westermann, *Theologie des Alten Testaments in Grundzügen* (ATD E6; Göttingen, 1978); J. Maier, *Geschichte der jüdischen Religion. Von der Zeit Alexanders des Grossen bis zur Aufklärung* (Berlin, 1972); M. Hengel,

Judaism and Hellenism: Studies in Their Encounter in Palestine *during the Early Hellenistic Period,* tr. by J. Bowden, 2 vols. (Philadelphia, 1974); W. Bousset and H. Gressmann, *Die Religion des Judentums im späthellenistischen Zeitalter* (HNT 21; Tübingen, 1926[3]; 1966[4]). For the *description and history of institutions,* cf. R. de Vaux, *Ancient Israel: Its Life and Institutions,* tr. by J. McHugh (New York, 1961).

71. For the concepts of *oral* and *written tradition,* cf. below, p. 32ff.

72. The reader must pardon the lack of terminological consistency; cf. above, pp. 22–23.

73. On this, cf. K. Elliger, *Leviticus* (HAT 1, 4; Tübingen, 1966), pp. 10ff. and 26ff.

74. On this, cf. A. H. J. Gunneweg, *Leviten und Priester* (FRLANT 89; Göttingen, 1965), and A. Cody, *A History of Old Testament Priesthood* (AnBib 35; Rome, 1969).

75. Cf. R. P. Merendino, *Das Deuteronomische Gesetz* (BBB 31; Bonn, 1969), pp. 57ff.

76. Cf. also H. Ringgren, "Literarkritik, Formgeschichte, Überlieferungsgeschichte," ThLz 91 (1966): 641ff., especially 647: "We must always ask what a theory would look like when applied to the real order; in other words, whether it can be regarded as practical."

77. Cf. S. Ullmann, *A Linguistic Approach to Meaning* (Oxford, 1957). Ullmann begins his book with a discussion of terminology.

78. Cf. above, n. 24.

79. Cf. the Old Testament contributions in G. Kittel's *Theological Dictionary of the New Testament,* tr. by G. Bromiley (Grand Rapids, 1964–76); the *Theological Dictionary of the Old Testament,* ed. by G. J. Botterweck and H. Ringgren, tr. by J. T. Willis et al. (Grand Rapids, 1974–. Three volumes have appeared as of 1979). Finally, there is the more concise two-volume *Theologisches Handwörterbuch des Alten Testaments,* ed. by E. Jenni and C. Westermann, 1 (Munich and Zürich, 1971), 2 (1976).

80. On this, cf. Ullmann, op. cit.

81. Cf. above, n. 36.

82. J. H. Hospers (ed.), *A Basic Bibliography for the Study*

of the Semitic Languages 1 (Leiden, 1973), 2 (1974), covers the whole area of the Semitic languages and cultures, and as such should be on the desk of every Old Testament scholar. Hospers also indicates the bibliographical resources for each subject area.

Deserving of express mention are: F. Stier and Eleonore Beck (eds.), *Internationale Zeitschriftenschau für Bibelwissenschaft und Grenzgebiete* (Stuttgart, 1952; Düsseldorf, 1954–); the *Elenchus bibliographicus* of the periodical *Biblica,* which until volume 48 was part of the periodical itself, but since volume 49 (1968) has been published separately; and *Old Testament Abstracts* (Washington, D.C., 1978–). The review section of the *Zeitschrift für die Alttestamentliche Wissenschaft* (ZAW) is indispensable because it reports so quickly on new books and recent periodicals. It is matched now by the *Zeitschrifteninhaltsdienst Theologie* (ZID), published since 1965 by the theological section of the Library of the University of Tübingen. Groups of books are reviewed in *Theologische Rundschau* (ThR) and in the Supplements to *Evangelische Theologie* that have been appearing under the title *Verkündigung und Forschung.*

In addition to the relevant professional journals, there are reviews in the *Book List* of the British Society for Old Testament Study, sometimes published in book form; in *Theologische Literaturzeitung* (ThLZ), now appearing in its 104th volume (1979), the *Theologische Revue* (ThRv), and (as representative of all the periodicals that review books in Oriental studies) the *Orientalische Literaturzeitung* (OLZ).

In addition to ZAW (for which there are two index volumes covering volumes 1–50 [1932]), *Vetus Testamentum* (VT), the publication of the International Organization for the Study of the Old Testament, is a periodical that covers the whole of Old Testament scholarship. Some periodicals covering both Testaments are the North American *Journal of Biblical Literature* (JBL), the French *Revue Biblique* (RB), the Roman *Biblica* (Bibl), the North American *Catholic Biblical Quarterly* (CBQ), and, as an example of an annual, the *Annual of the Japanese Biblical Institute* (AJBI; since 1975).

It should be noted that articles on the Old Testament appear more or less regularly in the general theological journals. Hospers's

Basic Bibliography indicates the periodicals that deal with the Semitic and ancient Near Eastern disciplines and institutions and that are important for Old Testament study. The whole of Egyptology is covered in the *Annual Egyptological Bibliography* of J. J. Janssen, which in its most recent volume (Leiden, 1978) reaches to 1974 in its reporting.

83. Some examples: J. Becker, *Gottesfurcht im Alten Testament* (AnBib 25; Rome, 1965), and T. Donald, "The Semantic Field of 'Folly' in Proverbs, Job, Psalms and Ecclesiastes," VT 13 (1963): 285ff.

84. On this, cf. J. Barr, *The Semantics of Biblical Language* (Oxford, 1961), p. 3.

85. Cf. Kaiser, *Introduction.*

86. My interpolation.

87. Kayser, *Das Sprachliche Kunstwerk,* p. 56.

88. Cf. above, pp. 26ff.

89. Cf. F. Huber, in G. Fohrer (ed.), *Exegese des Alten Testaments,* pp. 99ff.

90. In this sense, M. Noth's *A History of Pentateuchal Traditions,* tr. by B. W. Anderson (Engelwood Cliffs, N.J., 1972), provides the basis for his presentation of the corresponding periods in his *The History of Israel,* tr. by S. Godman (New York, 1960²). But cf. the critique of Noth's presuppositions in J. van Seters, *Abraham in History and Tradition* (New Haven, 1975), and in Kaiser, *Introduction.*

91. Cf. especially his *Psalmenstudien* II (Kristiania, 1922; reprint ed., Amsterdam, 1961).

92. Cf. I. Engnell, *Critical Essays on the Old Testament,* ed. by J. T. Willis and H. Ringgren (London, 1970), and, in addition, H. Ringgren, in ThLZ 91 (1966), 645–46, and Kaiser, *Introduction.*

93. Cf. H. Ringgren, "Literarkritik, Formgeschichte, Überlieferungsgeschichte," ThLZ 91 (1966): 641ff.

94. Cf., e.g., the discussion of the hypothesis that in the period before Israel became a state it existed as an amphictyony: from the initial proposal of the hypothesis, through the extensive defense of it by M. Noth, *Das System der zwölf Stämme Israels* (BWANT 4, 1; Stuttgart, 1930; reprint ed., Darmstadt, 1966), to the first

attack, which drew new attention to the problem, by G. Fohrer, " 'Amphiktyonie' und 'Bund'?'' ThLZ 91 (1966): 801ff., also in his *Studien zum altetstamentlichen Theologie und Geschichte* (BZAW 115; Berlin, 1969), pp. 84ff., and finally to O. Bächli, *Amphiktyonie im Alten Testament* (Basel, 1977). Or cf. the debate over the connection between covenant and law, which finally led to a late date being assigned to the introduction of the entire concept of covenant by S. Mowinckel, *Le Décalogue* (Paris, 1927); this was followed by A. Alt, "The Origins of Israelite Law" (1934), in his *Essays on Old Testament History and Religion,* tr. by R. A. Wilson (Oxford, 1966), and G. von Rad, *The Problem of the Hexateuch* (1938), tr. by E. W. Trueman Dicken (New York, 1966). As an example of the supplementary hypothesis, introduced after the Second World War, that the Israelite covenant formula was based on the formula for treaties between states in the ancient Near East cf. G. E. Mendenhall, *Law and Covenant in Israel and the Ancient Near East* (originally in BA, 1954, pp. 26–46 and 49–76; in book form: Pittsburgh, 1955); the above-mentioned objection of Fohrer; the semantic protest of E. Kutsch, summarized in *Verheissung und Gesetz. Untersuchungen zum sogenannten "Bunde" im Alten Testament* (BZAW 131; Berlin, 1972); L. Perlitt, *Bundestheologie im Alten Testament* (WMANT 36; Neukirchen, 1960); and D. J. McCarthy, *Treaty and Covenant* (AnBib 21A; Rome, 1978[2]).

For discussion of A. Alt's hypothesis regarding Israelite law, cf. Kaiser, *Einleitung*[4], pp. 64ff., which on p. 29, n. 5, and pp. 68ff also goes into the two problems just mentioned and gives fuller bibliography. For discussion of research on the prophets, compare, e.g., the approach based on the history of literary tradition as represented by E. Rohland, *Die Bedeutung der Erwählungstradition Israels für die Eschatologie der alttestamentlichen Propheten* (Heidelberg dissertation, 1956), with the approaches taken by G. Wanke, *Die Zionstheologie der Korachiten* (BZAW 97; Berlin, 1966), and O. Kaiser, "Geschichtliche Erfahrung und eschatologische Erwartung," NZSTh 15 (1973): 272ff., also in *Eschatologie im Alten Testament,* ed. by H. D. Preuss (WdF 180; Darmstadt, 1978), pp. 444ff., and idem, *Isaiah 13–39* (Philadelphia, 1974). Or compare the role assigned to the covenant by, e.g., Weiser,

ATD 20–21 (Göttingen, 1952, 1977[6]), or H. Graf Revetlow, BZAW 82 (Berlin, 1962), or Kaiser, ATD 17 (Göttingen, 1963[2] [1978[4]]), with the reservations of Kaiser, ATD 18 (1976[2]) and the discussion in R. E. Clements, *Prophecy and Tradition* (Atlanta, 1975), especially pp. 8ff.

95. The continuity of research in the history of religions has been ensured, in German Old Testament scholarship, chiefly by Otto Eissfeldt. The fruits of his work are to be found not only in his basic monographs but in his *Kleine Schriften,* ed. by R. Sellheim and F. Maass, I–V (Tübingen, 1962–73).

For an example of how observations in the history of religions can compliment one another and undermine a whole chain of constructions in the history of literary tradition, see the works, which appeared almost simultaneously, of R. Rendtorff, "El, Ba‘al und Jahwe. Erwägungen zum Verhältnis von kanaanäischer und israelitischer Religion," ZAW 78 (1966) 277ff., also in his *Gesammelte Studien zum Alten Testament* (ThB 57; Munich, 1975), pp. 172ff., and G. Wanke, *Die Zionstheologie der Korachiten* (BZAW 97; Berlin, 1966). Cf. also O. Kaiser, "Geschichtliche Erfahrung und eschatologische Erwartung" (n. 94, above).

96. Cf. n. 47, above.

97. Cf. the relevant sections in the introductions listen in nn. 26, 27, and 30, above.

98. Cf. the works listed in n. 70.

99. Cf. above, p. 22ff. The relevant presentations are listed in Hospers, *Basic Bibliography,* except for Egypt. For a general introduction to the modes of thought of the ancient Near Eastern and Egyptian worlds, cf. H. and H. A. Frankfort, J. A. Wilson, and Th. Jacobsen, *The Intellectual Adventure of Ancient Man* (Chicago, 1946). For the material environment, cf. the *Kulturgeschichte des Alten Orients,* ed. by H. Schmökel with the collaboration of H. Otten, V. Maag, and Th. Beran (Stuttgart, 1961).

For an introduction to Egyptian religion and culture, cf. H. Frankfort, *Ancient Egyptian Religion* (New York, 1948), and E. Otto, *Wesen und Wandel der ägyptischen Kultur* (Verst ändliche Wissenschaft 100; Berlin, Heidelberg, and New York, 1969). As reference works, cf. H. Kees, *Der Götterglaube im Alten Ägypten* (Berlin, 1956[2]); S. Morenz, *Egyptian Religion,* tr. by A. E. Keep

(London, 1973); H. Bonnet, *Reallexikon der ägyptischen Religionsgeschichte* (Berlin and New York, 1971²). Further bibliography is given in J. J. Janssen (ed.), *Annual Egyptological Bibliography* (Leiden, 1948ff.).

For a basic overall presentation of the ancient Mesopotamian world, B. Meissner, *Babylonien und Assyrien* I (Heidelberg, 1920), II (1925), is still indispensable. A presentation that reflects the present state of scholarship and takes account of the specialization that has developed since Meissner's time is given by S. N. Kramer, *The Sumerians* (Chicago, 1963), and A. L. Oppenheim, *Ancient Mesopotamia* (Chicago, 1964). For bibliography, cf. R. Berger, *Handbuch der Keilschriftliteratur* I-III (Berlin, 1967–75); for further information, cf. the *Reallexikon der Assyriologie und vorderasiatischen Archäologie* (RLA), founded by E. Ebeling, B. Meissner, and E. Weidner and now edited by D. O. Edzard (Berlin, Leipzig, and, later, New York, 1928ff.); the fascicles of volume 5 are now (1979) appearing.

For the history of Iranian religion, cf. G. Widengren, *Die Religionen Irans* (RM 14; Stuttgart, 1965). The needed references for Islam may be found in Hospers, *Basic Bibliography,* vol. 2.

H. Gese's contribution to H. Gese, M. Höfner, and K. Rudolph (eds.), *Die Religionen Altsyriens, Altarabiens and der Mandäer* (RM 10, 2; Stuttgart, 1970), must henceforth be regarded as a basic work on the immediate religious environment in which the people of the Old Testament found themselves. Gese gives, e.g., a detailed description of the myths of Ugarit. Periodicals especially concerned with questions about Syrian–Canaanite religion are: *Syria* (Paris, 1920–) and *Ugarit-Forschung* (UF) (Kevelaer and Neukirchen, 1969–). The entire area that concerns us is dealt with in H. W. Haussig (ed.), *Wörterbuch der Mythologie* I. *Götter und Mythen im Vorderen Orient* (Stuttgart, 1965).

Important collections of texts for the study of ancient Near Eastern literature, religion, and secular history are: K. Galling (ed.), *Textbuch zur Geschichte Israels* (TGI) (Tübingen, 1968²); H. Donner and W. Röllig, *A Synoptic Concordance of Aramaic Inscriptions* (Missoula, Mont., 1975); H. Gressmann (ed.), *Altorientalische Texte zum Alten Testament* (AOT) (Berlin and Leipzig, 1926²); J. B. Pritchard (ed.), *Ancient Near Eastern Texts*

Relating to the Old Testament (ANET) (Princeton, 1955[2]), together with the supplement: *The Ancient Near East* (Princeton, 1969), which also contains additions to J. B. Pritchard (ed.), *The Ancient Near East in Pictures Relating to the Old Testament* (Princeton, 1954). A good book for students is W. Beyerlin (ed.), *Near Eastern Religious Texts Relating to the Old Testament,* tr. by J. Bowden (Philadelphia, 1978); another is D. W. Thomas (ed.), *Documents from Old Testament Times* (London, 1958; New York, 1961).

Some general reference works are: the relevant volumes of the *Handbuch der Altertumswissenschaft,* founded by I. v. Müller, expanded by W. Otto, and presently edited by H. Bengston (HAW) (Munich), and the *Handbuch der Orientalistik,* ed. by B. Spuler et al. (HO) (Leiden).

An introduction to the history of religions is given by E. Dammann, *Grundriss der Religionsgeschichte* (ThW 17; Stuttgart, 1978[2]). Among more comprehensive works, we may mention the *Lehrbuch der Religionsgeschichte,* founded by Ch. de la Saussaye and edited by A. Bertholet and E. Lehmann, I–II (Tübingen, 1925[4]), and the *Handbuch der Religionsgeschichte,* ed. by J. P. Asmussen et al., I–II (Göttingen, 1971ff.). Relations between theology and the science of religions are investigated in contributions by theologians and scientists of religion, in U. Mann (ed.), *Theologie und Religionswissenschaft* (Darmstadt, 1973). Here H. Schmid and O. Kaiser deal with the ties between the Old Testament and its surrounding world in terms of the history of religions.

100. For questions of method, cf. also U. Bianchi, *The History of Religions* (Leiden, 1975). A critical report on "patternism" as applied to one area of Old Testament study is given by K. H. Bernhardt, *Das Problem der alttestamentlichen Königsideologie im Alten Testament* (VTS 8; Leiden, 1961).

101. Cf. the relevant works of G. van der Leeuw, *Religion in Essence and Manifestation,* tr. by J. E. Turner (London, 1938; 2nd German ed., 1956); K. Goldammer, *Die Formenwelt des Religiösen* (Stuttgart, 1960); F. Heiler, *Erscheinungsformen und Wesen der Religion* (RM 1; Stuttgart, 1961); G. Widengren, *Religionsphänomenologie* (Berlin, 1969); and also J. Wach, *Sociology of Religion* (Chicago, 1944).

102. On this point, cf. Heiler, op. cit., pp. 433–34.

103. Cf. M. Noth, *Die israelitischen Personennamen im Rahmen der gemeinsemitischen Namengebung* (BWANT 3, 10; Stuttgart, 1928; reprint ed., Hildesheim, 1966); J. J. Stamm, *Die akkadische Namengebung* (MVÄG 44; Leipzig, 1939; reprint ed., Darmstadt, 1968); H. B. Huffman, *Amorite Personal Names in the Mari Texts* (Baltimore, 1965); Frauke Gröndahl, *Die Personennamen der Texte aus Ugarit* (StP 1; Rome, 1967); F. L. Benz, *Personal Names in the Phoenician and Punic Inscriptions* (StP 8; Rome, 1972). For an introduction to the subject, cf. the relevant articles in the various dictionaries of the Bible; for example, the *Biblisch-Historisches Handwörterbuch* (BHW), ed. by B. Reicke and L. Rost, I–III (Göttingen, 1962ff.), the *Calwer Bibellexikon*, ed. by Th. Schlatter (Stuttgart, 1967²), or the *Bibel-Lexikon*, ed. by H. Haag (Zürich and Cologne, 1968²). Since the student of the Old Testament occasionally needs to go back to classical sources, I may mention here the *Oxford Classical Dictionary*, edited by N. G. L. Hammond and H. H. Scullard (Oxford, 1970²).

104. This is given in fact by the entries in the Hebrew lexicons and the dictionaries of the Bible.

105. Cf. above, n. 57. For a basic introduction to the world of Israel, cf. M. Noth, *The Old Testament World*, tr. by V. I. Gruhn (Philadelphia, 1966); K. H. Bernhardt, *Die Umwelt des Alten Testaments* I (Berlin and Gütersloh, 1967); D. J. Wiseman (ed.), *Peoples of Old Testament Times* (Oxford, 1973). Indispensable for a basic study of the historical setting is the *Cambridge Ancient History*, in which vols. I–IX cover the Old Testament period (I, 1–2, and II, 1, are in their 3rd ed.). Still useful is A. Scharff and A. Moortgat, *Ägypten und Vorderasien im Altertum* (Munich, 1950).

J. Finegan, *Handbook of Biblical Chronology* (Princeton, 1964), provides an introduction to Old Testament chronology, and E. J. Bickermann, *Chronology of the Ancient World* (London, 1968), to the chronology of antiquity. The special problem of the chronology of the monarchy in Israel is treated by, e.g., J. Begrich, *Die Chronologie der Könige von Israel und Juda* (BHTh 3; Tübingen, 1929); A. Jepsen and R. Hanhart, *Untersuchungen zur israelitisch-jüdischen Chronologie* (BZAW 88; Berlin, 1964) (also takes up the problems of the later period); and K. T. Andersen, *Die Chronologie der Könige von Israel und Juda* (StTh 23; 1969), pp. 69ff. The student will be helped by the conversion tables in R. A. Parker and W. H. Dubberstein, *Babylonian Chronology* (Providence, 1965), for the period from 626 B.C. to A.D. 75 Finally, I may mention the specialized presentations of W. Helck, *Geschichte des alten Ägyptens* (HO 1, 3; Leiden, 1968); F. K. Kienitz, *Die politische Geschichte Ägyptens vom 7. bis zum 4. Jahrhundert vor der Zeitwende* (Berlin, 1953); and H. Schmökel, *Geschichte des Alten Vorderasiens* (HO 2, 3; Leiden, 1957).

106. An introduction to the geography of Palestine is given by M. Noth, *The Old Testament World,* pp. 1–48 (basic questions of historical geography are treated in the same work in pp. 49–104), and D. Baly, *The Geography of the Bible* (New York, 1974²). For more complete presentations, and as reference books, cf. Y. Aharoni, *The Land of the Bible* (London, 1967); F.-M. Abel, *Géographie de la Palestine* I–II (Paris, 1933ff.; reprint ed., 1967³); and J. Simons, *The Geographical and Topographical Texts of the Old Testament* (Leiden, 1959). The authors of more recent Bible atlases complain a great deal about the lack of an up-to-date basic map that would include the modern place and area designations that are indispensable for the identification of biblical place names, especially in scholarly discussion. From this point of the view, the Bible atlas of H. Gauthe (Leipzig, 1926) continues to be, for the time being, indispensable. Among more recent atlases, special mention may be made of the *Oxford Bible Atlas,* ed. by H. G. May et al. (Oxford, 1974²), as suitable for ordinary use. Also useful is Y. Aharoni and M. Avi-Yonah, *The Macmillan Bible Atlas* (New York, 1977²). For further help in the identification of biblical places with their modern counterparts, the student may be referred to M. Noth, *Das Buch Josua* (HAT 1, 7; Tübingen, 1953²), pp. 142ff. In varying degrees, the lexicons and biblical dictionaries contain relevant entries.

For detailed maps, cf. the old *Survey of Palestine,* the *Survey of the Hashemite Kingdom of Jordan,* and the *Survey of Israel,* and the *Atlas of Israel* (Berlin and New York, 1973), as well as the Tübingen *Atlas des Vorderen Orients,* which will appear shortly.

107. For an introduction, cf. the *Geography* volume of the

Israel Pocket Library (Jerusalem, 1973); E. Orni and E. Efrat, *Geography of Israel* (Jerusalem, 1971); and, among older works, H. Guthe, *Landeskunde Palästinas* (Monographien zur Erdkunde 21; Bielefeld and Leipzig, 1927³).

As a resource for folklore study, G. Dalman, *Arbeit und Sitte in Palästina* I–VII (Gütersloh, 1928ff.; reprint ed., Hildesheim, 1964), is still indispensable. It may be supplemented by R. J. Forbes, *Studies in Ancient Technology* (London, 1964ff.), of which 11 volumes have thus far been published.

108. Cf. I. Benzinger, *Hebräische Archäologie* (Tübingen, 1907²); P. Volz, *Die Biblischen Altertümer* Stuttgart, 1925²); and F. Nötscher, *Biblische Altertumskunde* (Bonn, 1940).

109. Two basic books are: W. F. Albright, *The Archaeology of Palestine* (Baltimore, 1961²), and K. M. Kenyon, *Archaeology in the Holy Land* (London, 1965²). Concrete supplementary information may be found in D. W. Thomas (ed.), *Archaeology and the Old Testament* (Oxford, 1967). H. J. Franken and C. A. Franken-Battershill, *A Primer of Old Testament* (Leiden, 1963), can serve as a methodological introduction to the reading of excavation reports. An introduction to the concrete practice of field work is provided in the *Vademecum der Grabung Kamid el-Loz,* ed. by R. Hachmann (Saarbrücker Beiträge zur Altertumskunde 5; Bonn, 1969). The *Handbuch der Archäologie* (HA) includes U. Hausmann (ed.), *Allgemeine Grundlagen der Archäologie* (Munich, 1969). An indispensable reference work is: K. Galling, *Biblisches Reallexikon* (HAT 1, 1; Tübingen, 1937) (BRL¹), and its complete revision in 1977².

For questions of architecture, R. Naumann, *Architektur Kleinasiens* (Tübingen, 1971²), can be profitably used until works on more specific areas appear. C. Wattzinger, *Denkmäler Palästinas* I–II (Leipzig, 1933–35), is likewise still useful, although since its publication biblical archaeology has made immense strides; this progress was inevitably reflected only partially in A. G. Barrois, *Manuel d'archéologie biblique* I–II (Paris, 1939 and 1954).

For help in the area of pottery, cf. R. Ameran, *Ancient Pottery of the Holy Land* (Jerusalem, 1969).

Reports on excavations and research can be found especially in *Biblical Archeologist* (BA), the *Bulletin of the American Schools of Oriental Research* (BASOR), the *Annual of the Department of Antiquities of Jordan* (ADAJ), the *Israel Exploration Journal* (IEJ), *Levant,* the *Palestine Exploration Quarterly* (PEQ), the *Revue Biblique* (RB), *Syria* (Syr), and the *Zeitschrift des Deutschen Palästina Vereins* (ZDPV).

On the problem of the further historical use of archaeological findings, cf. M. Noth, "Der Beitrag der Archäologie zur Geschichte Israels," VTS 7 (Leiden, 1960), pp. 262ff., also in *Aufsätze zur biblischen Landes- und Altertumskunde,* ed. by H. W. Wolff, I (Neukirchen, 1970), pp. 34ff.

110. Cf. H. W. Wolff, *Anthropology of the Old Testament,* tr. by M. Kohl (Philadelphia, 1974). More specialized studies that are particularly relevant are: A. R. Johnson, *The Vitality of the Individual in the Thought of Ancient Israel* (Cardiff, 1964²), and L. Wächter, *Der Tod im Alten Testament* (Berlin and Stuttgart, 1967).

111. Cf., e.g., J. G. Droysen, *Outline of the Principles of History* (Boston, 1970), and, on the problem of evidence, W. Stegmüller, *Metaphysik, Skepsis, Wissenschaft* (Berlin, Heidelberg, and New York, 1969²), pp. 162ff.

112. Cf. above, p. 26f.

113. In principle, other approaches, such as the economic and sociohistorical, are part of the historical; they represent specific elements in the historical approach. Cf. the survey of research in W. Schottroff, "Soziologie und Altes Testament," VuF 19 (1974, no. 2): 46ff. In approaching the Old Testament from the standpoints of economic history and economic theory, the theologian will be helped by W. Eucken, *The Foundations of Economics* (London, 1979), to be clear in his terminology and to avoid stereotyped ideas.

There is urgent need of methodical reflection on the possibilities and limitations of approaching Old Testament texts in psychological and psychoanalytic terms. Cf. my remarks in *Introduction.* The reader may be referred to C. G. Jung, *Answer to Job,* in *Psychology and Religion: East and West,* tr. by R. E. C. Hull (Collected Works XI; New York, 1958), and to two further essays: J. Scharfenberg, *Sigmund Freud und seine Religionskritik* (Göttingen, 1968), and P. Ricoeur, *Freud and Philososphy: An Essay on Inter-*

pretation, tr. by D. Savage (New Haven, 1970). A. Vergote's essay, "Ein Beitrag der Psychoanalyse zur Exegese. Leben, Gesetz und Ich-Spaltung im 7. Kapitel des Römerbriefs," in X. Léon-Dufour (ed.), *Exegese im Methodenkonflikt* (Munich, 1973), pp. 73ff., must be left for evaluation to the student of the New Testament.

114. Cf. E. A. Nida and C. R. Taber, *The Theory and Practice of Translation* (Leiden, 1969), and A. R. Hulst, *Old Testament Translation Problems* (Leiden, 1960).

115. E. Hirsch, *Umformung des christlichen Denkens in der Neuzeit* (Tübingen, 1938).

116. Cf. above, pp.3-4.

NOTES FOR NEW TESTAMENT EXEGESIS

1. R. Bultmann, "Das Problem der Hermeneutik," ZThK 47 (1950): 51, reprinted in translation in *Essays, Philosophical and Theological,* tr. by J. C. G. Greig (London, 1955). The whole essay is well worth reading. Cf. also G. Ebeling, "Hermeneutik," RGG III,[3] p. 528, and the review of the history of the hermeneutic problem that is given in this article.

2. The 25th edition, which appeared in 1963, has since been reprinted without change; a new edition is being prepared that will be very different in many respects but will also be more practical. *The Greek New Testament,* which appeared in 1966 under the auspices of the major Bible societies, is meant primarily for use in translating the New Testament into the living languages of today; it offers more numerous witnesses than Nestle–Aland for the variants selected, but it is also more difficult to use and not always adequate. The Greek–Latin edition of Nestle is to be recommended highly (the Latin text is that of the official Vulgate with the divergences in the modern critical text of the Vulgate being given in the apparatus); the Greek–German edition (with Luther's version) should not be used for exegesis.

3. Suitable for students are: (*a*) the somewhat more comprehensive treatments by F. G. Kenyon and A. W. Adams, *The Text of the Greek Bible* (London, 1958), and B. M. Metzger, *Chapters in the History of New Testament Textual Criticism* (Leiden, 1963); (*b*) the shorter treatment in Introductions to the New Testament (cf. n. 7, below) and in H. Zimmermann, *Neutestamentliche Methodenlehre* (Stuttgart, 1967), pp. 31ff. Cf. the articles "Bibelhandschriften des NT" and "Textkritik II" in RGG I[3], pp. 1171ff. and VI[3], pp 716ff. (by G. D. Kilpatrick and H. Greeven), and "Bibel-

handschriften II'' and "Bibeltext II'' in LThK II², 352ff. and 372ff. (by H. J. Vogels and J. Schmidt).

4. H. G. Liddell, R. Scott, and H. S. Jones, *A Greek–English Lexicon,* 2 vols. (Oxford, 1940), with a *Supplement,* ed. by E. A. Barber (Oxford, 1968); *A Greek–English Lexicon of the New Testament and Other Early Christian Literature,* an edition and adaptation of W. Bauer's lexicon, by W. F. Arndt and F. W. Gingrich (Chicago, 1957); 2nd ed., revised and augmented by F. W. Gingrich and F. W. Danker from Bauer's 5th ed. of 1958 (Chicago, 1979).

5. C. F. D. Moule, *An Idiom Book of New Testament Greek* (Cambridge, 1959²); D. Tabachovitz, *Ergänzungsheft zu Blass-Debrunner* (Göttingen, 1965¹²).

6. Especially to be recommended in U. Wilckens, *Das Neue Testament übersetzt und kommentiert* (Zürich and Hamburg, 1970).

7. To be considered here are, on the one hand, the more comprehensive introductions that contain wide-ranging bibliographies: W. G. Kümmel, *Introduction to the New Testament,* rev., ed., and tr. (from the German ed. of 1973) by H. C. Kee (Nashville, 1975; there is a later revised and expanded German ed. of 1978); A. Wikenhauser and J. Schmid, *Einleitung in das Neue Testament* (6th ed., rev., Freiburg, 1972), and an English translation of the earlier 2nd edition: *New Testament Introduction,* tr. by J. Cunningham (New York, 1958); Ph. Vielhauer, *Geschichte der urchristlichen Literatur. Einleitung in das Neue Testament, die Apokryphen und die Apostolischen Väter* (Berlin and New York, 1975); H.-M. Schenke and K. M. Fischer, *Einleitung in die Schriften des Neuen Testaments* I. *Die Briefe des Paulus und Schriften des Paulinismus* (Gütersloh, 1978). On the other hand, there are shorter introductions, such as: W. Marxsen, *Introduction to the New Testament: An Approach to Its Problems,* tr. by G. Buswell (Philadelphia, 1968); E. Lohse, *Die Entstehung des Neuen Testaments* (Stuttgart, 1972; 1975²); H. Conzelmann and A. Lindemann, *Arbeitsbuch sum Neuen Testament* (Tübingen, 1975), 3. Teil; R. H. Fuller, *A Critical Introduction to the New Testament* (London, 1971²); N. Perrin, *The New Testament: An Introduction* (New York, 1974).

8. For the basis of this view and a survey of other solutions to the Synoptic problem, cf. Kümmel, op. cit., § 5. For the most

recent literature, cf. R. H. Fuller, "Die neuere Diskussion über das synoptische Problem," ThZ 34 (1978): 123ff.

9. Surveys of work in redaction criticism are given in: J. Rohde, *Rediscovering the Teaching of the Evangelists*, tr. by D. M. Barton (Philadelphia, 1968); H. Zimmermann, *Neutestamentliche Methodenlehre* (Stuttgart, 1966), pp. 214ff.; R. H. Stein, *What is Redaktionsgeschichte?* (London, 1969); J. Roloff, *Neues Testament* (Neukirchener Arbeitsbücher; Neukirchen and Vluyn, 1977), pp, 31ff.; N. Perrin, *What Is Redaction Criticism?* (Philadelphia, 1969).

10. The three fundamental works on the form criticism of the Synoptics are: M. Dibelius, *From Tradition to Gospel*, tr. by B. D. Woolf (1934); R. Bultmann, *The History of the Synoptic Tradition*, tr. by J. Marsh (1963); and K. L. Schmidt, *Der Rahmen der Geschichte Jesu* (1919; 1964[2]). Whoever cannot work through any of these books should at least acquaint himself with the basic insights of form criticism, using, for example, E. V. McKnight, *What Is Form Criticism?* (Philadelphia, 1969), or the relevant sections of Conzelmann and Lindemann, op. cit., pp. 67ff., or Roloff, op. cit., pp. 14ff., or of the Introductions to the New Testament.

11. There is a brief justification of this view in my essay "Das Problem des geschichtlichen Jesus in der gegenwärtigen Forschungslage," in my volume *Heilsgeschehen und Geschichte* (Marburg, 1965), pp. 392ff. Cf. also my *Jesu Antwort an Johannes den Täufer. Ein Beispiel zum Methodenproblem in der Jesuforschung* (Wiesbaden, 1974), pp. 132ff. (also in *Heilsgeschehen und Geschichte* II [Marburg, 1978], pp. 180ff.).

12. C. H. Bruder, *Tamieion . . . sive Concordantiae omnium vocum Novi Testamenti Graeci* (Göttingen, 1913[7]), and W. F. Moulton and A. S. Geden, *A Concordance to the Greek Testament* (Edinburgh, 1963[4]). Eight fascicles (containing about half of the vocabulary) have thus far appeared of a concordance that will satisfy every requirement: *Vollständige Konkordanz zum griechischen Neuen Testament. Unter Zugrundelegung aller modernen kritischen Textausgaben und des Textus Receptus* (Berlin, 1977–). This work will doubtless be brought to a speedy conclusion. The completed second volume (1978) contains specialized tables and will hardly interest beginners.

13. O. Schmoller, *Handkonkordanz zum Neuen Testament* (Stuttgart, 1968[14]). Another useful aid is the index volume for the Catholic *Regensburger Neues Testament*, scil. *Deutsches Wörterbuch zum Neuen Testament nach dem griechischen Grundtext*, by G. Richter (1962), since the passages relevant to a particular concept are given here in full (in German) and organized according to subject.

14. *Theological Dictionary of the New Testament*, tr. by G. Bromiley; nine volumes plus an index volume (Grand Rapids, 1964–76).

15. *Calwer Bibellexikon* (Stuttgart, 1959[5]); above all, the *Biblisch-historisches Handwörterbuch*, ed. by B. Reicke and L. Rost, 3 vols. (Goöttingen, 1962–66); of lesser importance, K. Galling (ed.), *Biblisches Reallexikon* (Tübingen, 1977[2]). Also useful is K. Matthiae, *Chronologische Übersichten und Karten zur spätjüdischen und urchristlichen Zeit* (Stuttgart, 1978).

16. O. Michel, in *Meyer's Kritisch-exegetischer Kommentar über das Neue Testament* (Göttingen, 1963[12]; 1966[13]); E. Käsemann, in *Handbuch zum Neuen Testament* (Tübingen, 1974[13]); H. Schlier, *Der Römerbrief*, in *Herder's Theologischer Kommentar zum Neuen Testament* (Freiburg, Basel, and Vienna, 1977). This choice of commentaries on the basis of methodical or theological diversity does not mean that other more recent commentaries are less valuable. This is certainly not true of O. Kuss, *Der Römerbrief übersetzt und erklärt*, 1st fascicle (Regensburg, 1957), and U. Wilckens, *Der Brief and die Römer* 1. *Röm 1–5* (Evangelisch-Katholischer Kommentar zum Neuen Testament; Einsiedeln–Cologne and Neukirchen–Vluyn, 1978). See also the list of commentaries in Kümmel, *Introduction*, pp. 305ff.

17. Schenke and Fischer, op. cit. (n. 7, above), pp. 136ff., and Wilckens, op. cit. (n. 16, above), pp. 27ff.

18. If doubts have been raised about the originality of the context in which a text has come down to us (e.g., according to widely held views, in the Corinthian and Philippian epistles), the exegete must endeavor to form his own opinion about the original context of the text and, in general, to ask whether another context can be found that has a better claim to be original. At all events, the interpreter must have clearly in mind whether he intends to interpret the

text as a component part of its traditional context, of some hypothetical context, or as having no discoverable original context.

19. See the names in Kümmel, *Introduction,* § 19, 1, and also in Wilckens, op. cit., pp. 15ff., 18ff.

20. Käsemann lists the witnesses to this variant.

21. On methodological grounds, the consultation of other commentaries is to be avoided here, although such consultation is quite possible and in many cases helpful.

22. It should be noted that Schmoller's concordance is not simply a mechanical listing of the occurrences of all words, but that it has them sorted into gorups (thus, e.g., under *eirēnē* its occurrences in the introductory passages in Paul's epistles and in the formula "God of peace" are grouped together). For this reason one must take care not to overlook occurrences of a word that may have been listed earlier in an article and also, if circumstances warrant it, one should critically examine the grouping to which Schmoller has assigned a particular occurrence of a word.

23. Here too B. Metzger's text-critical commentary on the Greek New Testament will prove instructive.

24. I add two points that the student may not find out on his own: that E. Haenchen in his commentary on Acts (Oxford, 1971), p. 140, n. 8, gives an exhaustive list of such passages (among them he puts Romans 5:2) and that the *Vollständige Konkordanz* (n. 12, above) makes it easy to check the combination of *kai* with a relative pronoun inasmuch as it lists all the occurrences of *kai.*

25. A glance at Blass and Debrunner's *Grammar* (§§ 341 and 342, n. 4) shows that *hestēka* has present meaning.

26. If one refers to the passage cited, Psalm 5:12, in Rahlfs's edition of the Septuagint, one finds *en* in the text and *epi* in the apparatus, which shows that the two prepositions were interchangeable after *kauchasthai.* An edition of the Septuagint is as valuable for the exegesis of the Old Testament as it is for understanding the language of the New Testament.

27. Here a glance at the margin of Nestle informs us that Romans 3:23 speaks negatively of the loss of *doxa,* whereas Romans 8:18 likewise speaks of the expectation of *doxa* for the eschatological future.

28. Above all, the article on *pneuma* in TDNT VI, especially

pp. 415ff. (E. Schweizer; further references are given there to works on New Testament theology and the theology of Paul).

29. Consultation of TDNT (II, 214ff.; G. Schrenk, and I, 172ff.; J. Behm) confirms these observations. Let me add a point that the student will not necessarily learn from using the commentaries: that the investigation of Paul's use of *en* by F. Neugebauer, *In Christus* (Göttingen, 1961), pp. 34ff., especially p. 43, shows that we have here a characteristic Pauline use of *en* in the sense of an "adverbial modification."

30. H. Strack and P. Billerbeck, *Kommentar zum Neuen Testament aus Talmud und Midrasch* III (1926), 223ff. This work is not a commentary in the ordinary sense, but a comprehensive collection of Jewish parallels to all ideas and customs in the New Testament that could have a Jewish origin. Good index volumes now also make it possible to find out the exact wording of rabbinical texts cited in this work only by abbreviated references.

31. Perhaps EKL III, 1652f.; RGG VI³, 1371ff.; CBL, 1361f.; R. Bultmann, *Theology of the New Testament*, tr. by K. Grobel, 2 vols. (New York, 1951–55), I, § 33; H. Conzelmann, *An Outline of the Theology of the New Testament*, tr. by J. Bowden (New York, 1969); cf. also Käsemann and the bibliography he gives on p. 124.

32. Further help can be gotten from Kuss's commentary (n. 16, above) in the excursus on pp. 213ff.

33. E. Klostermann, in *Handbuch zum Neuen Testament* (Tübingen, 1927²; 1971⁴); E. Schweizer, in *Das Neue Testament Deutsch* (Göttingen, 1973; 1976¹⁴); J. Schmid, in *Regensburger Neues Testament* (Regensburg, 1965⁵). Klostermann is purely historical and critical, Schweizer radically critical and radically theological, and Schmid Catholic and critical. On Mark, see E. Lohmeyer, in *Kritisch-exegetischer Kommentar zum Neuen Testament* (Göttingen, 1951¹¹ with supplemental brochure; 1967¹⁷); V. Taylor, *The Gospel according to Mark* (London, 1952); R. Pesch, in *Herder's Theologischer Kommentar zum Neuen Testament* (Freiburg, Basel, and Vienna, 1976). Lohmeyer is moderately critical, Taylor conservative, and Pesch Catholic and critical. On Luke, see E. Klostermann, in *Handbuch zum Neuen Testament* (Tübingen, 1929²; 1975³); W. Grundmann, in *Theologischer Kommentar zum*

Neuen Testament (Berlin, 1963; 1977[8]); K. H. Rengstorf, in *Das Neue Testament Deutsch* (Göttingen, 1972[15]; 1975[16]). Klostermann is purely historical and critical, Grundmann critical and biblicist, and Rengstorf conservative. For English-speaking students, the commentaries in the Pelican series are useful: J. Fenton, *The Gospel of St. Matthew* (Baltimore, 1963); D. E. Nineham, *The Gospel of St. Mark* (Baltimore, 1963, 1969); G. Caird, *The Gospel of St. Luke* (Baltimore, 1963). See also bibliographies in the general introductory works listed above in n. 7.

34. The best at present is K. Aland (ed.), *Synopsis of the Four Gospels: Greek–English Edition* (Stuttgart, 1972), but the synopsis of A. Huck is still usable. An English-language synopsis, based on the RSV text, is B. H. Throckmorton (ed.), *Gospel Parallels: A Synopsis of the First Three Gospels* (New York, 1967[3]).

35. Cf. Taylor, *Mark,* pp. 237, 240–41. For the analysis of a Synoptic text, one will also always refer to Bultmann, *History of the Synoptic Tradition* (in our case, pp. 13–14), and, if the passage is treated there, to Dibelius's *From Tradition to Gospel* (in our case, pp. 222–23).

36. It is strongly recommended that the student impress upon himself the agreements and disagreements in the wording of the Synoptic Gospels by making appropriate underlining, with different colored pencils, in a copy of a Synopsis.

37. The historical questions, whether the demon exorcism, which is lacking in Mark, formed the original introduction to the narrative, and why Matthew, contrary to his own doublet in 9:32–34 and contrary to Luke 11:14, speaks of a blind *and* dumb demoniac, are both important for critical study of the tradition, but do not contribute to the understanding of the Matthean text.

38. TDNT II, 1ff., and VII, 151ff., both by W. Foerster.

39. It is the same in profane Greek as one can see from Liddell and Scott (n. 4, above), p. 1927, under II, 2, and IV, 1.

40. This question is very difficult to decide.

41. A glance at Bultmann's *History of the Synoptic Tradition* (as recommended in n. 35, above) will confirm this observation (cf. p. 14). Cf. also Schweizer.

42. Cf., e.g., E. Grässer, *Das Problem der Parusieverzögerung in den synoptischen Evangelien und in der Apostelgeschichte*

(Berlin, 1957; 1977³), p. 7; contrast, e.g., W. G. Kümmel, *Promise and Fulfillment: The Eschatological Message of Jesus,* tr. by D. M. Barton (Studies in Biblical Theology 23; Napersville, Ill., 1961), pp. 105–9.

43. Klostermann leaves the question unanswered; Schmid does not discuss the problem at all; Schweizer lists a number of possible interpretations but does not choose any one of them.

44. To be sure, if the commentaries used normally in one's exegetical work give no answer or no satisfactory answer to an individual problem, one will consult further commentaries and other literature about Jesus, Paul, etc. Whether any commentary whatever is successful in explaining the sense of Matthew 12:31–32 in the context of Matthew's Gospel is, to me, very doubtful. If one supposes the originality of Mark 3:28–29, the formation of the version of the saying in Q may nevertheless be understood as an expression by the Christian community of its differing attitudes toward the human Son of man, on the one hand, and the Risen Christ, active in the Spirit, on the other. Further discussion of the antiquity and original meaning of Mark's version of the saying may be found in Bultmann, *History of the Synoptic Tradition,* pp. 403–4, and in the most recent works on the Son of man problem: H. E. Tödt, *The Son of Man in the Synoptic Tradition,* tr. by D. M. Barton (Philadelphia, 1965), pp. 118–20, 312–18; F. Hahn, *The Titles of Jesus in Christology,* tr. by H. Knight and G. Ogg (Cleveland, 1969), pp. 293–94; A. J. B. Higgins, *Jesus and the Son of Man* (London, 1964), pp. 127ff.; F. H. Borsch, *The Son of Man in Myth and History* (London, 1967), pp. 315, 328. The student will not find the last two titles in the commentaries I am using here. However, he will find further literature listed in Pesch, pp. 220–21, and in G. Schneider, *Das Evangelium nach Lukas: Kap. 11–24* (Ökumenischer Taschenbuchkommentar zum Neuen Testament; Gütersloh, 1977), p. 277.

45. See Bauer–Arndt–Gingrich's *Lexicon,* p. 688, under β.

46. Well-founded theories about the history of the tradition of this text are to be found in Bultmann, *History of the Synoptic Tradition,* pp. 74, 83–84. If no extensive treatment of the analysis of such a text can be found in works on form criticism, the student should also survey other literature about Jesus and, in the case at

hand, works about the parables and the ethical teaching of Jesus in particular. Here may be mentioned A. Jülicher, *Die Gleichnisreden Jesu* II (Tübingen, 1898; 1910[2]); J. Jeremias, *The Parables of Jesus*, tr. by S. H. Hooke (New York, 1963[6]), pp. 90, 92; E. Neuhäusler, *Anspruch und Antwort Gottes* (Düsseldorf, 1962), pp. 56–57.

47. Cf. Jülicher, op. cit., p. 126.

48. So too Schweizer. Cf. also (not listed in the commentaries and lexicons): J. Jeremias, *New Testament Theology: The Proclamation of Jesus*, tr. by J. Bowden (New York, 1971), and W. G. Kümmel, in *Heilsgeschehen und Geschichte* (Marburg, 1965), p. 386.

ABBREVIATIONS

AASF	*Annales academiae scientiarum Fennicae*
ADAJ	*Annual of the Department of Antiquities of Jordan*
AJBI	*Annual of the Japanese Biblical Institute*
AKM	*Abhandlungen für die Kunde des Morgenlandes*
AnBib	*Analecta Biblica*
ANET	*Ancient Near Eastern Texts Relating to the Old Testament*, ed. J. B. Pritchard
AOT	*Altorientalische Texte zum Alten Testament*, ed. W. Gressmann
ATD	*Das Alte Testament Deutsch*
BA	*Biblical Archaeologist*
BASOR	*Bulletin of the American Schools of Oriental Research*
BBB	*Bonner Biblische Beiträge*
BHTh	*Beiträge zur historischen Theologie*
BHW	*Biblisch-historisches Handwörterbuch*
Bibl	*Biblica*
BRL	*Biblisches Reallexikon*, ed. K. Galling
BWANT	*Beiträge zur Wissenschaft vom Alten und Neuen Testament*
BZAW	*Beihefte zur Zeitschrift für die alttestamentliche Wissenschaft*
CBL	*Calwer-Bibellexikon*
CBQ	*Catholic Biblical Quarterly*
EHS. T.	*Europäische Hochschulschriften*. Reihe 23: *Theologie*
EKL	*Evangelisches Kirchenlexikon*
FRLANT	*Forschungen zur Religion und Literatur im Alten und Neuen Testament*
HA	*Handbuch der Archäologie*

HAT	*Handbuch zum Alten Testament*
HAW	*Handbuch der Altertumswissenschaft*
HNT	*Handbuch zum Neuen Testament*
HO	*Handbuch der Orientalistik*
IEL	*Israel Exploration Journal*
JBL	*Journal of Biblical Literature*
KAI	*Kanaanäische und aramäische Inschriften*, eds. H. Donner and W. Röllig
LThK ²	*Lexikon für Theologie und Kirche*, 2nd ed.
MVÄG	*Mitteilung en der Vorderasiatisch-Ägyptischen Gesellschaft*
NTD	*Das Neue Testament Deutsch*
NZSTh	*Neue Zeitschrift für die systematische Theologie*
OLZ	*Orientalische Literaturzeitung*
PEQ	*Palestine Exploration Quarterly*
RB	*Revue biblique*
RGG ³	*Die Religion in Geschichte und Gegenwart*, 3rd ed.
RLA	*Reallexikon der Assyriologie und vorderasiatischen Archäologie*
RM	*Die Religionen der Menschheit*
StP	
Syr	*Syria*
TB	Taschenbuch (-bücher)
TDNT	*Theological Dictionary of the New Testament*
TGI	*Textbuch zur Geschichte Israels*, ed. K. Galling
ThB	*Theologische Bücherei*
ThLZ	*Theologische Literaturzeitung*
ThR	*Theologische Rundschau*
ThW	*Theologische Wissenschaft*
ThZ	*Theologische Zeitschrift*
UF	*Ugarit-Forschung*
UTB	*Uni-Taschenbücher*
VT	*Vetus Testamentum*
VTS	*Supplements to Vetus Testamentum*
VuF	*Verkündigung und Forschung*
WdF	*Wege der Forschung*
WMANT	*Wissenschaftliche Monographien zum Alten Testament*

ZAW	*Zeitschrift für die alttestamentliche Wissenschaft*
ZDPV	*Zeitschrift des deutschen Palästinavereins*
ZID	*Zeitschrifteninhaltsdienst Theologie*
ZThK	*Zeitschrift für Theologie und Kirche*

Exegetical Method

Now revised and completely updated, this importan
text for the beginning student and seminarian is once
again available. Written by two internationally known
German biblical scholars, this book has been a standard
reference book in Europe and America since the 1960s
The material covered gives concise descriptions of al
the critical methods used by biblical exegetes today, and
clear directions for students to use these methods or
their own to become equipped to decide for themselve
among the many conflicting opinions about textua
problems in the Bible. Otto Kaiser covers the basic skills
needed for the Old Testament, and Werner Kümme
those needed for the New Testament.

THE SEABURY PRESS · NEW YORK

ISBN: 0-8164-

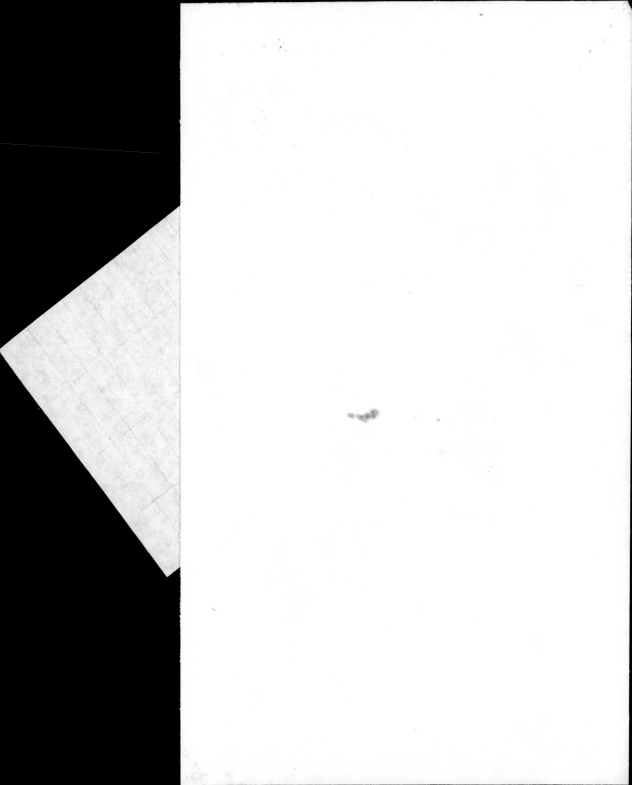

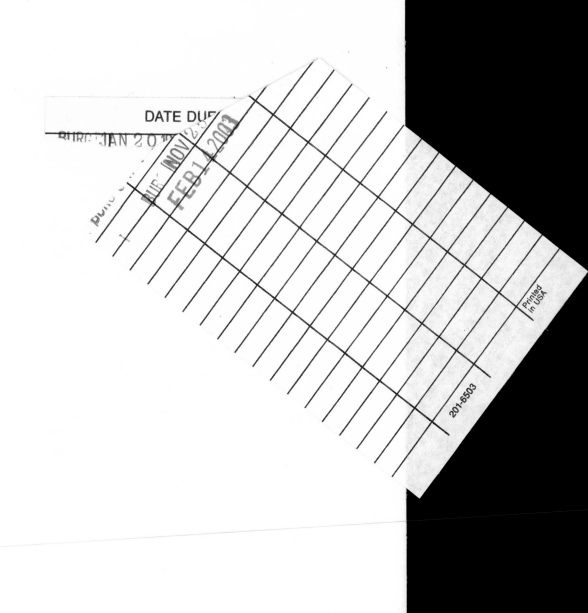